BONGO BONGO BONGO
I DON'T WANNA
LEAVE THE
CONGO
VERONICA CECIL

A Memoir

KWELA BOOKS

Kwela Books,
an imprint of NB Publishers,
40 Heerengracht, Cape Town, South Africa
PO Box 6525, Roggebaai, 8012, South Africa
www.kwela.com

Cover design by Michiel Botha
Author photograph by Sam Reinders
Map by Bennie Krüger
Typography by Nazli Jacobs
Set in Accolade
Printed and bound by Paarl Print,
Oosterland Street, Paarl, South Africa

First edition, first impression 2009

ISBN: 978-0-7957-0282-2

To David and our children

Preface

I can see it quite clearly. I am outside the store at Elizabetha. It is a dull brick building with a tin roof, one of a rash of European dwellings and offices in a clearing of the plantation above the river. The heat lolls in an air heavy with moisture. In the distance I can hear a patter of drums. Twelve people are being lined up against the wall. Ten whites. Two blacks.

One of the whites is the Portuguese trader. He is a small man with a beer belly and bad teeth, but such spirit. It isn't just his money and his colour that have made him a king; it is his sexual prowess. Even in extremis he carries himself with a certain swagger.

Then there are the nuns. I can hardly bear to think of them. Fluttering, broken birds, this may be their chance to become martyrs, to return in triumph to their Maker. But how can they hold their heads up when they have been violated? Wimples awry, they form a confused heap of black and white, like seagulls on an oil-polluted beach.

The old planter and his wife are another thing. Vieux colons, old colonials. Living here so long they have become weather-beaten, intertwined with one another and the jungle. They could face even this catastrophe with equanimity, were it not for the child. That is the part that is unbearable. She should be at boarding school in Europe, but she is still young – too young for parents of their age. She arrived unplanned and has become so precious they cannot bear to part with her. One of the planter's arms is crooked round her head, which he clasps to his chest, while the other holds her body. All the captors can see is a neat back parting and two thick blonde plaits. His wife stands beside him. She has grey hair neatly pulled back into a bun. Straight and still she is, as she has always been, the rock in adversity.

In contrast, the young planter who lived down-river is in hysterics. He is a nouveau colon. He holds his two-year-old child up at the rebels, shaking her and shouting hysterically until he gets knocked in the mouth with a rifle and collapses in a heap. His young wife is already down on the ground. Mute with shock, she is on her knees. She doesn't even hear her child crying any more. She lifts her head and a silent scream rips the air.

It is the black men, however, that I am most troubled about. Not the rebels – they are drug-crazed, faceless extensions of a gun – but the two Ghanaians. They have stirred up something more complex than pure horror. I see them dressed improbably in torn suits and grubby ties. How else would we know that they are ordinary businessmen caught up in a mess that has nothing to do with them? For the past few weeks they have been trying to escape through the jungle, sleeping beside the mosquito-infested river, hacking their way through the mangrove swamps. They speak no Lingala. Their limbs are stippled with sweat, and the blood has drained from their faces like the colour from a badly dyed garment. As far as they're concerned, these rebels – who call themselves Simbas, lions – are savages. Young men, barely into manhood, they are doped up with dagga and primitive superstitions. As soon as they were captured, the Ghanaians knew they were doomed. Not only are they foreigners in an alien country, they are middle-class businessmen working for a European corporation. This makes them worse than whites.

How could I have imagined that I'd leave the Congo unscathed? That I could simply jet in, live a dream, and jet out again? But then, come to

think of it, I hadn't. I'd wanted to be involved. Wanted to make a difference. What I hadn't imagined was that it would all turn out the way it
did.

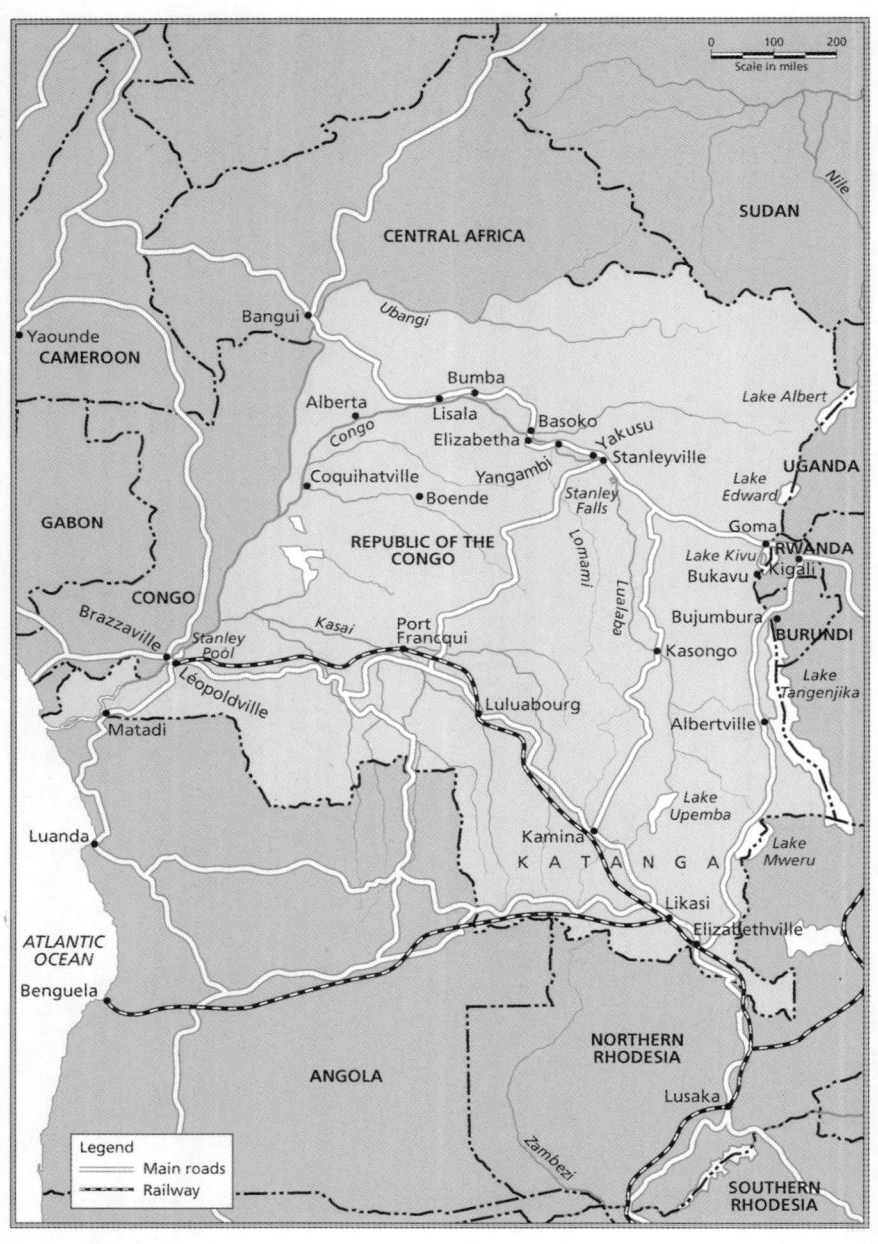

PART I

Chapter 1

It was a dank February evening when David, in starched collar and tie, arrived home to a flat draped with nappies and felted-up matinée jackets, to announce that the Company had suggested sending him to the Congo. I didn't want to go. Instant visions of mangrove swamps and mosquitoes flooded my mind. Followed by images of disease, death and disaster. The Congo was the armpit of Africa. At the same time, I knew that questioning the Company's decision would be futile. This was the early Sixties, when employees fell in with their bosses' wishes. And wives did as they were told.

Ever since he'd joined the Company we'd known that David would be sent abroad. We were looking forward to it. He had left his safe job as a chartered accountant to join the burgeoning world of big business. "We comb the country," the Company chairman had boasted in one of the Sunday newspapers, "for the cream of Britain's young brains and talent." David was known as a management trainee. He was one of the chosen. We'd envisaged a high-status job in New York or Sydney – which had recently become fashionable. But the Congo? What was there for a future captain of industry to do in the Congo?

"They want me to reconstruct their accounting systems," David said rather grandly. "Make long-term financial forecasts. Bring the whole thing up to date."

"What about Charles?" Charles was our small baby.

"Oh, he'll be fine. The Company has its own clinic and there are plenty of trained doctors out there." The Company, he assured me, would look after us in every way. They'd provide us with housing, a car, even a large hamper of food, chosen by us and shipped out every six months. We would live in luxury. David had never travelled beyond Europe, and I was beginning to sense that he viewed the idea of going to Africa as a bit of an adventure.

"And," he added, playing his trump card, "they pay half my salary in Congolese francs and half in sterling. We should be able to live on the Congolese francs and save the sterling."

That was the clincher. There may have been plenty of kudos in being a management trainee, but the pay was low. We couldn't even afford proper heating.

The winter of 1962/63 has, rightly, gone down in history. It started with the smog. A large wad of cotton wool descended on London, making it impossible to see more than a few feet in front of our faces. Traffic was brought to a standstill and David struggled off to work with a gauze nappy tied across his face. The cattle brought up to London for the Smithfield Show died in their stalls, and there was a red alert at all the hospitals – old people and babies were particularly vulnerable. I holed myself up with Charles, who was only a few months old. Even then, the pollution in the flat was so bad that a saucer of ammonia left on a dresser was neutralised within an hour.

The fog was followed by a cold so intense that it, too, has become legendary. A permanent film of ice had formed inside the kitchen window and icicles hung over the sink. The only faint warmth came from a pathetic gas contraption, and an electric heater with one bar. I may have been a Spartan by nature but even my capacity for endurance was being seriously challenged. I'd forgotten what it felt like not to be cold. On the other hand, quite apart from disease, I did not want to go back to Africa.

Rhodesia, where my parents had decided to settle when I was ten years old, may have been warm, but it was a cultural desert. And there was also the racial question.

Up till its independence, I'd lived in India and then, after a brief spell in England, my family moved to Southern Rhodesia in 1948. After the austerities of post-war rationing, the food, the light, the feeling of space, and, above all, the freedom to be a child again, had felt truly wonderful. But, even as a ten-year-old, I'd been vaguely troubled by the relationship between black people and us. Our servants in India, while admittedly still servants, had been our friends and mentors, substitute parents, even. In the Southern Rhodesia of 1948, most Africans were, it seemed, automatically "munts' and "kaffirs". My moment of epiphany came when our "houseboy" Joseph told me he'd seen me in town. I realised then that I'd never looked at his face.

My older brother, who came out to join us a few months later fresh from his English preparatory school, dealt with this racial unease by tackling it straight on. He was a brilliant mimic and I remember coming into the kitchen to find an audience of Joseph, the gardener Job and a couple of "piccanins" – probably Joseph's children – literally falling about in mirth as he re-enacted, in the accent of the locals, a scene between my mother and her houseboy. My mother was castigating Joseph for stealing the sugar. My brother played both parts. He'd often entertained our Indian servants in the same way, earning himself the lifelong nickname of Joker.

It was at the posh girls' boarding school in South Africa that everything I had sensed uneasily about race began to fall into some sort of logical sense. My guru was a maths teacher called Mrs Roux. She was married to an Afrikaner and was passionate not only about her subject but also about politics. "I will not talk small talk," she flared when an

15

unfortunate girl asked her what she'd done in the holidays. "What is the point of being alive if you don't care about the condition of the world you live in and the people around you?" Ideas were everything. She was a feminist, an atheist and, above all, a champion for the rights of black people.

No one growing up in 1950s Southern Africa could have been unaware of the racial question. It was intrinsic to the privileged, balmy air we basked in. History, however, was shifting. India had been granted its independence and, as the British prime minister was to put it later, the wind of change had already started to blow through Africa. But the year we arrived, in 1948, apartheid became law in South Africa. A glass wall came down to divide white opinion. Liberals on the one side, diehards on the other. Sophiatown in Johannesburg was bulldozed and pass laws were introduced, which meant that black people had to carry identity cards and were restricted to the areas where they lived and worked. In response to these iniquities, some of the liberal whites acted with astonishing bravery. Even ordinary housewives, the mothers of my school friends, stuck their necks out by putting on black sashes and convening in small groups at public functions to protest, passively and mutely, against the death of the democratic rights of coloured voters.

It was impossible not to be stirred and invigorated by the gusts and eddies of the times. By the age of eighteen, I knew I had a moral choice to make. The right one, of course, would have been to stay in South Africa and fight for the rights of black people, but . . . but . . . I wanted to get on with my life. I couldn't wait to leave school and go overseas. It wasn't my problem, I rationalised. I'd lived only half my life in Africa. And in any case, what real effect would I have? South Africa, everyone predicted, would one day turn into a blood bath. I pictured a rising tide of crimson sea flooding the country. I didn't want to die young. When my parents told me they weren't prepared to pay for university in South Africa, my dilemma was decided. They wanted me to become a secretary, and although I wasn't too keen on the idea, at least it entailed a one-way ticket to England.

The England of 1956 should have been a gloomy place. Post-war rationing had only just ended, taxes were high and the lifestyle austere. But I fell in love with the country of my forebears. I didn't even care about the weather. I had been given a chance to reinvent myself and London, I discovered, was brimming with ideas about art and theatre and philosophy. I was poor, but then so was everyone else I made friends with. It was the very lack of money that I found most liberating. Most people in England were far poorer than the average white settler in Rhodesia. Indeed, the ostentatious wealth was one of the things I'd disliked about colonial Africa – though it was the lure of money that had accounted for the wave of immigration, including my own family's, after the war. Even the fact that I was hopeless at shorthand and typing didn't matter. It was a stopgap and England gave me the opportunity to go on the stage. My family back in Africa were horrified, but I didn't care.

By the time I met and fell in love with my husband, I'd been acting for a couple of years and in the words of Charlotte Brontë's Jane Eyre: "Reader, I married him." He was a conventional husband, and I did my best to become a conventional wife. David was everything I admired about English men: thoughtful and kind, as well as gentle and generous. He was a historian, and he shared my love of literature. Although he was, at heart, an intellectual – he'd been offered a scholarship at Cambridge – he'd trained as a chartered accountant for practical reasons in order to make a good living His venture into the world of business was a challenge. He was ambitious and I was ambitious for him. We were a team.

When I met David I'd still thought of myself as the little colonial girl.

17

Marrying him had made me feel properly English. I went on to give birth to an English baby. If I did ever think about the country I had been brought up in, it was from a safe distance. I had abandoned for ever, or so I thought, the person I had been in Africa. David's announcement that the Company wanted to send him to the Congo demolished this carefully constructed person in one go. It was as if I'd been confronted with the self I'd been at such pains to get rid of. But, as the idea of returning to Africa seeped into my consciousness, I found myself warming to it more and more. It wasn't just the weather. The Congo was not the same as Rhodesia and South Africa. It was a newly independent country. Black people had been given their freedom. They could determine their own future. I pictured a country of happy, smiling people. I would love them, and they would love me.

What I conveniently managed to overlook was the fact that there had been internal turmoil ever since those very people had been given their autonomy in June 1960. Independence had been followed by chaos, and Belgian paratroopers had been called in to quell the rebels. They had been followed by a United Nations Peacekeeping force. The eastern province of Katanga had seceded from the rest of the Congo because of its mineral wealth. The result had been an undignified flight of many of the whites, who included some of my friends, into neighbouring Rhodesia.

Then, in January 1961, Patrice Lumumba, the Congo's first democratically elected prime minister, was murdered. That should have rung warning bells. But at the time I barely took it in. I was newly married and Africa was somewhere else. Faced with the prospect of actually going to the place, I managed to persuade myself that the troubles were mere teething problems. I needed to hold on to my vision of a brave new Congo, a place of peace and harmony, with, of course, racial equality. I truly believed that all you had to do was to give African countries their independence and everything would turn out all right in the end.

As our venture started to take shape, both David and I found ourselves getting increasingly excited. Although we were to start off in the capital Léopoldville, while David reconstructed the accounts system, the eventual plan was to move upcountry to the interior. There he would be in charge of the finances of one of the Company's palm oil plantations.

"They're huge," he said. "Each one is like a mini-kingdom." He made it sound like a fairy story. "And you needn't worry about Charles," he added. "Every station has got its own doctor."

I wasn't worried. Not any more. I believed David when he assured me that the Company would look after us.

"Oh Bongo Bongo Bongo, I don't wanna leave the Congo," I sang.

"What on earth's that?" David asked. We were scanning the catalogue, working out what we were going to order for our first hamper.

"It was *the* big hit when we first got to Southern Rhodesia," I explained. "Bingle Bangle Bungle, I'm so happy in the jungle, I refuse to go." I could almost hear the sound from a wind-up gramophone pounding through the netted window of one of the colonial bungalows in the little one-horse dorp we lived in.

"Don't want no bright lights, false teeth, doorbells, da-da, da-da, da-da-da-daa . . ."

"Shall I tick Marmite, then?"

"Oh, I'm sure we'll be able to get that. How about Patum Peperium?"

The plantations were situated along the Congo River. In the evenings we would pore over maps, fantasising about the new life opening up in front of us. In my imagination the mangrove swamps had started turning themselves into lush tropical jungles, and the mosquitoes vanished in orange sunsets over the river. In fact, I was so convinced that the life we were about to embrace was going to be new and exciting that not even Mr Clayton could shake my convictions.

Mr Clayton, a Company employee, had been sent to fill us in and tell us what to expect. "I only work there for the money," he said with laudable honesty. He was a Northerner who'd taken refuge in the Isle of Man to avoid tax. "My wife hates the place. She stays at home because of the children and their schooling."

I was shocked. I was a product of the British Empire. I believed that wives should stand by their husbands. Even if it meant wading through mangrove swamps, hacking my way through the Congolese jungle with my baby on my back, I'd be there.

"Why does she hate the place?" I asked Mr Clayton.

"You name it, she hates it."

"In what way?"

"She doesn't like the heat, or the food, or the people."

"Doesn't she like *anything* about it?"

"No."

We dismissed his testimony. Mr Clayton, I told David, still had the mentality of an exploitative colonialist, and his wife, who clearly didn't want to expand her horizons, was using the children as an excuse. Far from being put off by the Company's candid emissary, we decided that he'd made the venture seem like an exciting challenge. David was going to revolutionise the Company's accounting system, while I would stand stalwartly at his side. Behind every successful man was a woman. I pictured myself as a latter-day cross between Isabel Burton, loyal wife of the Victorian explorer Richard, and Mary Kingsley, intrepid explorer in her own right. I resolved to pour my energies not only into my husband, but also into the newly liberated Congo. I would get to know the locals and make friends with them. I would make a difference to their lives. In the dim recesses of my mind I imagined I would expiate my own cowardly past.

Chapter 2

Stepping out of the air-conditioned plane at Léopoldville was like entering a sauna. Rhodesia was on a plateau, and fairly dry. The atmosphere here was hot, heavy, tangibly wet, and it smelt of damp flannels. But to my ex-colonial eyes it seemed nothing short of a miracle that the khaki-clad officials were not only black, but also spoke French. They had their pride and their dignity. They were free. This was the new Africa that I had dreamed about.

"Passeport," one of them barked.

"Si, si." I scrabbled about in my handbag, and found it.

"What is the purpose of your visit?" he asked roughly. Or at least that's what I thought he asked.

"I am coming to join my husband," I said in my schoolgirl French. But he didn't seem to understand, and with his index finger kept stabbing at the passport and the form I'd filled in. We were stuck in this state of mutual miscomprehension when I spotted a wheyfaced David breaking through the crowds.

"Where the hell have you been?" David, normally the mildest of mild-mannered men, was clearly agitated.

"Didn't you get the telegrams?" I asked.

"No."

"I don't understand."

"I've met every single plane from Johannesburg for the last four days."

"I . . . I'm so sorry." The reason for our delay was so complicated I

22

couldn't even begin to explain. David gave me a sweaty kiss, took his son into his arms, and slipped the intransigent official a matabishe, a bribe. My passport was stamped and we were waved through.

David had been frantic with worry. He'd telephoned everyone he could think of, including, of course, my parents, who'd assured him that we'd set off on our journey. As far as he knew, we had simply disappeared off the face of the earth. And, in a way, we had.

It was partly his fault. He had flown out to the Congo ahead of me to get things ready while I'd gone to stay with my parents, now living and working in Iran. In every letter, he'd stressed that I mustn't forget to bring with me the necessary bottle of duty-free whisky. As my journey, the cheapest available, had meant flying from Iran to Léopoldville via Johannesburg, where we had to change planes, I'd decided to buy it during the brief stopover in Nairobi. The purchase had meant producing my passport.

Charles was by this stage nearly a year old. Having been cooped up for hours, he was naturally anxious to get moving. While I was buying the whisky, he'd taken the opportunity to investigate an alluring cigarette butt on the floor at the other side of the air terminal. He was a nifty crawler, and I had only just managed to retrieve him when the loudspeaker told passengers to get back on board. Grabbing the precious whisky, and with a squirming toddler in my arms, I made for the plane. As I looked down from the safety of the air into the crater of Mount Kilimanjaro and pictured the fiery inferno below, I remembered my passport. I had left it on the counter of the duty-free shop in Nairobi. In those days, air stewards went out of their way to be helpful. The pilot of the plane was alerted. He tried to make radio contact with Nairobi. We had just flown out of Kenyan airspace. Never mind, they assured me; everything would be fixed when we got to Johannesburg.

23

They did their best. I'd been allocated a gem of a woman, employed by El Al Airlines. She tried phoning Nairobi. They, it seemed, had shut up shop for the night. And Léopoldville was having its siesta. I couldn't just take the next flight back to Nairobi, pick up my passport, and return to Joburg, because the terms and conditions of my ticket forbad it. I was exhausted and Charles was frantic. From time to time I heard announcements over the loudspeaker telling the world that due to passenger problems the plane to Léopoldville would be delayed. Eventually, the plane took off without us.

Under any other circumstances nothing would have induced me to enter South Africa, especially Johannesburg, where I'd gone to school. But the alternative was flying straight back to Teheran and starting the journey all over again. I begged. I pleaded. I grovelled. The boot-faced South African official was intransigent. Without a passport, he insisted, there was no way I would be allowed into his country. Increasingly desperate, I pulled out every stop. So did my El Al lady. The final resort was bursting into tears. They were genuine. At last a crack began to appear. Other officials were summoned. They hummed and haw-ed interminably . . . Provided the airline would vouch for us, they said . . . The El Al lady assured them it would . . . On the other hand . . . A young mother with a child . . . Perhaps, under the circumstances . . . Finally, they conceded, and before anyone could change their minds, we were bundled into an overcrowded minibus. That was how Charles and I ended up staying – though admittedly in the cheapest room – at the most expensive hotel in Johannesburg.

Before leaving, the El Al lady assured me that she would send a telegram to my husband in Léopoldville. To make doubly sure, I went to the post office the next day and sent one myself. After that, as there was nothing to do but wait, I decided to ring up my old school friends. I also

24

contacted my ex-maths teacher, Mrs Roux, who visited me in my hotel room. She told me that she was now persona non grata. In fact, she was so non grata that the apartheid government had confiscated her passport. She explained that she was now a volunteer teacher, that she taught black people maths in the evenings. "Education is the only way to empower them," she declared, as ever cutting the small talk. I imagined her words coursing through the bugging system which, I was convinced, had been planted in the ceiling light.

Being in Joburg had catapulted me straight back into the muddled, guilt-ridden world of adolescence. As the days and nights passed fruitlessly by, I began to feel increasingly desperate. I pictured my passport being seized by the South African authorities. I remembered how, as a schoolgirl, I'd gone out for the day with a friend. She lived in a large Johannesburg house called Mon Repos. "People like you," her father had sneered when I'd spouted my views on the Nationalist government, "are dangerous." At the time I'd felt as if he'd taken a machete and sliced me to the ground. Now, back in Joburg, I felt much the same way. What matter that we liberals stood for democracy? Under the present regime we were non-people.

The cruel atmosphere of Joburg had worsened in the seven years since I'd left school. This was reflected in the bleak, high walls of the city and the bowed heads of the few blacks to be seen on the streets. Every time I left the hotel I was convinced that the shadowy presence of a secret policeman was following me. I became so paranoid that I stopped going out altogether. After four days, I'd persuaded myself that I would never see my husband again, that Charles and I were doomed to moulder away for the rest of our lives in the clutches of the Nationalist government, and that this fate was no more than I deserved. Then, at my lowest ebb, the El Al lady phoned to say that my passport had turned

25

up. It had been languishing in the pocket of a pilot who'd disembarked in Rhodesia and forgotten all about it.

It was strange seeing my husband in this bizarre setting. He seemed to have changed. There was a new confidence in him. Even though he still spoke rather touchingly in the accent of a schoolboy, his French sounded fluent, and he understood exactly what the official wanted. He took charge, handing the customs official another matabishe to get us through customs with no more questions; then he collected our luggage and summoned a porter. I noticed that he ordered the man around as if he'd lived in Africa for years. This was disconcerting, as one of the reasons I'd chosen David in the first place was that he was as far from the "rugger-buggers" of my youth as it was possible to be. Now, dressed in khaki shorts, Aertex shirt and long socks, he not only looked disconcertingly like them, he was behaving like them too.

On the plane I'd spoken to an American anthropologist who had worked with Professor Leakey in Kenya. This was something David was particularly interested in, so when I spotted Larry looking lost in the huge state-of-the-art terminal I introduced him to my husband. David, who had a Company car, offered him a lift into town.

It was beginning to get dark as we left the airport. In the half-light we were overtaken by an armoured car.

"What's that?" I asked.

"United Nations Peacekeeping," David said, as if this were perfectly ordinary.

"But there isn't a war?"

"Adoula has asked for UN soldiers in order to deal with Katanga." Cyrille Adoula was the new president instated by the West after the Lumumba assassination.

"I thought Katanga was on the other side of the country." Our map-studying had not been for nothing. Léopoldville – which would later be called Kinshasa – was on the west side of the Congo, Katanga in the east.

"There's a man called Moïse Tshombe," David explained, "who's leading the breakaway faction and refusing to give Katanga back." It all sounded rather childish.

The sun sets fast near the equator and, within minutes, we were plunged into absolute darkness. The driver put his foot down. His headlights lit up the road, which was virtually deserted. Every now and again he swerved to avoid a pothole.

"Isn't he going a bit fast?"

"One has to. There are bandits out there."

"What?"

"They jump out of the bushes and stop the cars; then they hold the passengers up at gunpoint."

"Good God." This was from Larry, who was sitting in the front of the car beside the driver. David had made it sound very gung-ho and casual.

At that moment the car squealed to a halt. We stood there while a troop of frogs crossed the road. Their slimy bodies gleamed in the headlights.

I clung to my child as the car sped on through the darkness. What was I bringing him to? Then we arrived at the outskirts of the city. Here, there were at least signs of some sort of normality. The shacks beside the road were lit with lamps and there were fires with cooking pots. People moved about in the half-light. These were no bandits. They were the sort of Africans I knew and recognised.

Someone had said, or written, that Léopoldville was the "Paris of Africa". This had conjured up visions of European grandeur blended with the exotica of the tropics. And although the city, with its wide, neon-lit boulevards and high-rise blocks seemed somewhat soulless, the Memling, where Larry was staying, was everything I'd been hoping for. It was like a luxury hotel in Europe, a world away from the bandit-infested airport road and the shacks. Here, there was light and music, with whiffs of Gitanes and snatches of French conversation. Elegantly coutured guests in low-cut dresses and tuxedos decorated the foyer. There was even a black man in a dinner jacket – one of the new breed of multicultural sophisticates that I was about to get to know. In a corner, another black man was playing a white piano. The sound of nostalgic Forties music carried me into a world of half-remembered make-believe. I could have been in *Casablanca*.

We ordered our drinks and went outside to sit in the courtyard. Drops of water from a fountain caught the light as they rose and then fell into the darkness of the pool. Charles had fallen asleep in David's arms. While the men discussed skulls and Piltdown man, my mind drifted. I was still on a high from the excitement of finally getting here. Sitting under the African stars in balmy air heavy with the smell of jasmine, I felt relaxed and contented. The scent had wafted me back to 1948 and my first night in Africa.

We'd left poor, bruised, ration-restricted England on a wet February morning. Everything had been grey: grey pavements, grey skies, even people's overcoats had been grey. Our plane, not jet-propelled but driven by whirring propellers, had flown over the Sahara Desert. Underneath, the dunes had risen and fallen like waves on a vast yellow ocean. Descending to Khartoum in the Sudan in the middle of the night had been like landing not so much on a new continent as a new world. It wasn't only the warmth and the smells, it was the feeling of abundance. The Nile slid past the hotel like a monstrous black snake; waiters in red fezzes and starched uniforms produced a cornucopia of tropical fruit I'd never even seen before. Lychees, passion fruit and papayas. And, miracles of miracles after war-rationed England, as much bacon and egg and sausage as we could possibly eat.

Chapter 3

I suppose that, after all that build-up, our new home – the house where David and Charles and I were going to spend the next six months of our lives – was bound to come as a letdown. It was on the outskirts of Léopoldville, in a street lined, not with flowering jacarandas or flamboyants, but palm trees – the squat, ugly kind that grew everywhere like weeds. Our house was a small, modern bungalow, almost identical to the other bungalows lining the street. Although it had a veranda, there were no pots of hibiscus, no purple bougainvillea, no swags of coral creeper – none of the remembered extravagance of my childhood. It was strictly functional, with a carport and a small back garden. Not that I was aware of all of this when we arrived in the darkness. Nor was I aware of the block of flats which loomed up behind us. What hit me was the bleakness of the interior. The floors were concrete, the lights an unforgiving neon; the furniture was the dull utilitarian stuff my mother used to call "government furniture".

By this stage, David had completely forgiven me my much-delayed arrival and was bubbling with enthusiasm. He had only just moved in himself and he pointed out that the Company had had a cot specially made for Charles, and that we had the luxury of air conditioning. I tried to hide my disappointment.

"And this is the kitchen," he enthused, showing me into a room even more dreary than the rest. "I bought this fridge from Provis." Provis was David's Belgian predecessor. "He let me have it for a very good price . . ."

29

I thought the "very good price" was pretty steep.

". . . I wish you could have met him, you'd have loved him; he's got such a merry twinkle in his eyes . . ." I was pretty certain that Provis had taken David for a ride and that I wouldn't have loved him at all, but I didn't say so.

My lack of love turned into positive hatred the next morning when I discovered that we had no car. Provis had, apparently, crashed the one that went with the job. It was the car I would have used. There were no replacement parts so it couldn't be repaired. And new cars were like gold dust – I think those were David's words. My husband would be fetched and brought back every day by the Company driver, but, unless we bought a vehicle for ourselves – and they were hideously expensive – I would have to rely on lifts from other people.

We hadn't only bought his fridge, we had apparently inherited Provis's "boy" as well. Despite Independence, male servants were still known by the humiliating English term "boy". Females were "boyesses". The word "boy" was particularly inappropriate in the case of Francois, an elderly man with grizzly hair and a bony face. He didn't live in the back garden as the Rhodesian servants had, but came to work on his bicycle. I found him disconcertingly subservient.

"I'll send the Company car home to take you shopping," David said as he left for work. He'd assumed that I would enjoy being driven from shop to shop like an Edwardian lady, with someone to carry my parcels. And in many ways he was right. Although I disapproved in theory, there was a part of me that yearned for just that.

George, the driver, was young and fun and full of life. He kept up a stream of conversation in what seemed at the time to be almost incomprehensible French. He asked me all about Queen Elizabeth, and though I had to admit that we weren't acquainted, this didn't seem to worry him.

He tried football, a subject I was equally ill-informed about, but that didn't matter either. What did matter was that we liked one another and that he treated me as . . . well, almost, as an equal. But then, so he should. He was a free man, one of the newly liberated Congolese, part of the new world I was about to discover.

Seen in the daylight and from the outside, Léopoldville, as we drove through it, appeared still to be a very elegant city. In the latter days of colonialism, the Belgians must have spent a lot of money. Rather like the air terminal, Léopoldville was a late-Fifties-cum-Sixties state-of-the-art city. Modern blocks, built of stylish concrete slabs with decorative fretwork, lined the wide boulevards. What I was soon to discover was that this was all a façade; the interiors of those smart buildings were beginning to crumble like neglected teeth. Inside the modern supermarché, the tacky, new plastic surfaces were already chipping. The walls had acquired a grubby, neglected look. What really hit me, though, was that the whole shop looked as if a giant vacuum cleaner had sucked up its contents. Row after row of empty shelves stretched out like railway lines on either side of the aisles. They were dusty and desolate. Only one solitary row with large tins of dried milk broke the symmetry. It was America's surplus sent as aid. I bought several tins. I also rescued a rusty tin of pilchards, sitting alone and unloved. It had been there so long it left its brown mark on the shelf. There was no flour, no cereals, no fruit, or vegetables, no . . . anything. There wasn't even any soap powder.

"How do people live?" I asked George. He shook his head.

"C'est une vraie catastrophe," he said solemnly, and then, as if to indicate that I should not trouble myself with such things, he grinned. I was a visitor to his country.

The full impact of the catastrophe was brought home by a crowd of peo-

31

ple standing in a queue in the baking heat. George told me that they were waiting for a consignment of salt that was supposed to be coming in – or it may have been sugar, or flour. The air of resignation reminded me of the "natives" in the townships: lines of men waiting for bags of mealie meal. Suddenly there was an eruption, a near-riot as they shoved their way towards a door at the side. The consignment had arrived.

I pushed down a feeling of mild panic that was fluttering in my stomach. If basics were so hard to come by, how were we going to live? Then I reminded myself that we were white and employees of the Company. They would never let us starve. George, as if determined to prove this, drove me to a small shop in another part of the city; it was called Le Petit Pâtisserie.

"Voilà!" he exclaimed proudly.

The window was crammed full of pastries, with crystallised fruit on top and fluffy meringues oozing cream. It was just like one of those shops you see in Vienna, or, presumably, Brussels. To George's disappointment, I didn't buy anything. A single tart, by my calculations, cost a day's wages in African terms.

The question of vegetables was solved later that morning when a man came to the house with a basket containing a few scrawny lettuces, some onions and potatoes, and a small pile of French beans. "See, they're fresh," he said, snapping a bean in half with panache. "Voilà. Pas de ficelles."

"There must be some mistake," I said to Francois when the man weighed out some vegetables and asked for the money. The beans may not have been stringy, but they were alarmingly expensive.

"Non," Francois assured me. There was no mistake. That was what they cost. Reluctantly, I bought them. How were we going to save any money if vegetables cost ten times what they would have in London?

I'd never really experienced food shortages before. Apart from that year spent in England just after the war, I'd always lived in lands of relative plenty. And even then, the lack hadn't really affected me. My mother had fumed because our landlady, who was in charge of the coupons, was favouring another lodger. She kept kennels and had an unmarried daughter. The lodger, an innocent-looking organist from Oxford, was a bachelor. I knew the poor girl hadn't a hope. Apart from the fact that she smelt of dogs, he didn't look to me like the marrying kind.

"It's the children who need the food," my mother had ranted. Now I found myself feeling the same way. How was I ever going to be able to give Charles a proper diet? At least in post-war England there'd been a semblance of fairness. Here in the Congo it was dog eat dog.

"It's a barter economy," David's new friend Thoby, who came round that evening, explained cheerfully. "Provided you've got something someone else needs, you can get whatever you want." Thoby, who told me that his "daddy" was an Oxford don, was also a management trainee. He was in sales, which meant, he said – helping himself liberally to our duty-free whisky – that there were always spare packets of soap powder to be swapped for some desirable goody or other.

"But what have we got?" I couldn't imagine accountants getting those sorts of perks.

"Ah," Thoby smiled a trifle smugly, "you've got to cultivate the right people."

"Cultivate the right people? How?"

"We can always change our hard currency on the black market for seven times its value," David put in.

"I thought the whole point of coming out here was to save."

"Yes, but . . ."

"Seven times is still far more than you'd pay at home . . ."

"Mrs Van Royan will show you the ropes," Thoby cut in.

I knew I was being humoured. And I knew too that I could hardly blame David for the state of the country. But I couldn't help feeling that we had been deceived. It wasn't so much a bottle of whisky I should have missed a plane for, but a bag of flour.

Mrs Van Royan was a Dutch woman who was married to Thoby's boss, the sales director of the Company. She and her husband had befriended David before I arrived and it was she who had stocked up my larder with basic necessities. She visited me the next day. She was a large woman. Her hair was hennaed dark red, and she had baggy eyes set deep in one of those faces you know instinctively carry behind them layers of wisdom and experience. Packing me into her Volkswagen Beetle, she drove me off to see her butcher.

There was nothing in his shop except bare slabs of marble, but he did produce a bloody parcel from underneath the counter for Mrs Van Royan. There was, however, no meat to spare. He told me he would keep me in mind, but I doubted it. As Thoby had indicated the evening before, it wasn't just about money. Those who could offer something that was in short supply got the goodies.

"I have arranged for you to play bridge," Mrs Van Royan announced when we got back home. David had told her I was a player.

"I'm not sure that I can . . ." The idea of frittering away my mornings playing bridge appalled me. In England I'd been stuck in the flat with a small baby. My only intellectual stimulus had been my radio. Here, with a servant to wash up and clean and even cook, I was free to work. I'd decided, having become addicted to the radio, that I'd try my hand at journalism. I was determined to use my time in the Congo profitably.

"One of our ladies has gone away, so you will be able to play with us on Thursday mornings."

"I'm afraid I won't have the time."

"You will find that they are very nice ladies. Very friendly. I will fetch you at nine o'clock tomorrow and take you there in my car."

"What about Charles?"

"Your boy will look after him."

"But . . ."

"My friend Sannie, who plays bridge with us, has chickens."

"Oh?"

"She has more eggs than she can eat herself and she has promised me that she will sell you a box every week."

It didn't take much persuasion for me to capitulate. My first day in the Congo had shown me just how serious the food situation was. The Company may not actually have allowed its employees to starve to death – this, I realised, had been the purpose of the food hampers – but they certainly weren't going to mollycoddle us. We had to look after ourselves. As a large part of the European diet appeared to be tinned food, I was seriously worried about Charles. He was too old to exist on a diet of American powdered milk. And eggs were, after all, eggs. With nothing but my very dubious bridge skills to offer in exchange, I couldn't help acknowledging that it wasn't a bad bargain. Besides, I rationalised, it would allow me to get to know another nationality. Possibly even learn another language. Dutch was not so very different from Afrikaans, which I'd studied briefly at school.

The next morning, Mrs Van Royan duly turned up in her handy little Beetle and we set off. The ladies, it transpired, took turns to host the game and this week it was Sannie's turn. She lived further out of town – hence the chickens. It was a modern bungalow, a replica, I imagined, of her home in Vlaardigen, or wherever it was she came from. There was a three-piece suite covered in cut-moquette, swirly patterns on the carpets, and shiny wooden carvings of naked African women. The whole place was immaculately clean and polished.

The game was played in English for my benefit, and the Dutch women all spoke shamingly well. "You call it a yarborough when you have no picture cards, not so?" and "A small slam, that is when you get all the tricks except one?" When someone suggested I hold my cards closer to my chest, I told them my mother-in-law's joke about fine eyes being better than finesse. It took them a moment or two to work out the pun.

"Fine eyes are better than finesse. That is good. Very good. Ha, ha, ha."

After the first rubber, a servant came in with a trolley on which there was not only coffee, but also dainty cakes, and dainty plates to eat from, with dainty forks and dainty napkins. God knows where the ingredients had come from. Besides having chickens, Sannie, whose husband was also in sales, had clearly cultivated the right people. We all took a break while we chatted about this and that, and I had to admit that Mrs Van Royan was right. They were nice ladies. They were all older than me and their interests were purely domestic, but they made a real effort to make me feel one of the group. This certainly wasn't how I'd envisaged spending my time in the new Africa, but I was learning.

Chapter 4

In the summer of 1963 the *New York Times* described the state of affairs in the Congo as a "stagnant calm". Seen from a distant point of view, that was a pretty accurate description. Since the mineral-rich province of Katanga had broken away from the rest of the Congo, Cyrille Adoula, the puppet president installed by the West after Patrice Lumumba's assassination, had asked not only for money but UN troops also to deal with the situation. And yet, despite the troops and the millions of American dollars which had been poured into the country, nothing had been resolved. The Christian, missionary-educated Moïse Tshombe, who had won control of Katanga at Independence, had gone on to lead the secession. While Tshombe sat tight on his valuable minerals, Adoula stayed in Léopoldville, apparently twiddling his thumbs. And the West appeared to be impotent in doing anything about the situation.

Stagnant calm was also not a bad way of describing the life that David and I had settled into. It very soon became apparent that there was no way we were going to meet any black people socially. My sole contact with the indigenous Congolese was limited to my own and other people's servants. And it soon became clear that it wasn't going to be any easier getting to know the Belgians. Opposite us lived a couple called M and Mme Bossart. Monsieur was a Company man and, like David, worked in the accounts department. He was small and slight with a neat little moustache, and he reminded me of one of the male characters in a De Maupassant short story. Madame was of indeterminate age. She had

peroxided blonde hair and a voluptuous figure. She must have been giv-
en to getting up late because whenever I saw her she was dressed in a
satin dressing gown and mules with ostrich feathers. I had hoped
that by getting to know her, I would be able to improve my French, but
that was clearly out of the question. No neighbourly popping in; Mme
Bossart barely acknowledged my existence.

The centre of my social life, I soon discovered, was supposed to be the
Company club, La Maison de Passage, which was a short walk from our
house. It was where travelling employees stayed. Indeed, David had lived
there before I arrived. Besides the tennis courts – there was no swimming pool – it had the usual lounge and bar, as well as a large veranda
where people met up with their friends. But even at the club it became
apparent that the Belgians kept themselves to themselves. Certainly, the
women did. It was almost as if, because they'd been here first, they regarded themselves as some sort of elite. The people I was expected to
fraternise with were the other British wives.

I loathed clubs. Apart from the fact that I'd been an outsider, a despised
"pommy", the clubs in Rhodesia were where the locals would gather to
air their prejudices and shore up their certainties.

La Maison de Passage was no different. I soon discovered that most of
my fellow countrywomen, the wives with whom I was supposed to make
friends, had, by and large, adopted the same attitudes as the colonials
of my youth. The Congolese may not have been "munts" and "kaffirs",
but they were despised just the same. And here, there was even less reason. We were guests in this country, a country where black people were
now supposed to be in charge. How could we continue to regard ourselves as the superior race?

David, on the other hand, saw the whole setup in a completely different light. He had none of my colonial baggage. He'd written enthusiasti-

cally about the new people he'd met. In his letters he'd made them sound unusual and interesting. "They call the food 'chop'," he'd exclaimed in delight. To me, the word "chop" – I imagine, derived from "chopsticks" – sounded colonialist and patronising. But then David was properly English. He'd come with an open mind. The club had not only been the centre of his existence, it had been his introduction to Africa. And although to begin with he had been shy and selfconscious about his French, he was naturally good at sport, and by the time I arrived he'd made plenty of friends and was booked up for a game of tennis most evenings.

"It's the freedom," he said of his fellow males. "They don't have to dress up in a collar and tie and they don't have to take a train to work. Oh, they may grumble about Independence, and if you ask them why they're out here, they'll say the climate and, of course, the money. But if you press them, they'll admit that it's really the freedom they go for. They also like being part of a group, as well as being their own masters . . ."

David was, of course, talking about himself. And, put like that, I could understand it. I believed that he honestly hadn't given the racial aspect much thought, or if he had, he was prepared to swallow the whole package. And I hadn't been wrong at the airport. He had joined the club in more ways than one. The new way of life he'd been thrown into made him feel more powerful. He'd been automatically accepted because he was one of the chaps. Here, just as it had been in the colonies, it was a man's world and the genders were kept separate. The men in Rhodesia had bent over their beers at the bar, talking about their farms and the price of tobacco, or the affairs of state. The women had sat in another part of the room doing their knitting and gossiping about their servants. This was why I'd needed to escape from Africa in the first place. There may have been no tobacco or knitting – here they talked business – but the atmosphere in the Congo was the same.

Not that I eschewed the club altogether. That would have been impossible. At weekends David and I would play tennis, and I did my best to make friends with the mothers of toddlers so that Charles would have other children to play with. But I was also determined to do my own thing. Besides race, my maths teacher had taught me to question sexual stereotyping. I was determined not to fall into the cliché of the bored colonial housewife with nothing better to do than paint her nails and go to coffee parties. On the mornings that I didn't play bridge, or go shopping with George, I tapped away on the keys of my Olivetti portable typewriter while Charles played outside. We had a tiny garden which required little work, so the gardener, who was employed and paid by the Company, was quite happy to be a part-time nanny. He talked no French, but that didn't matter to Charles.

Although I enjoyed having servants and someone to do the housework, it wasn't only my fellow whites I was having problems relating to. I didn't really know how to treat Francois. By the time I arrived he and David appeared to have established a perfectly good, uncomplicated master–servant relationship. "Dites bonjour à Madame," he had apparently said to David while dusting a photograph of me on the bedside table – David had told me this in one of his letters and I'd had a warm glow of anticipation. Confronted with the real person, however, I couldn't feel quite the same way. Francois was polite enough on the surface – overpolite, in fact – but he was too glib, too charming, to be real. I felt uneasy with him. I was also inhibited by the fact that he was old enough to be my father.

David had assured me he'd come with glowing testimonials – testimonials no doubt written by Provis. "We're really lucky to get him," David assured me. "Everyone in Leo's after him." Francois's only drawback, it seemed, was his six children, and by law employers had to pay extra for every child of an employee. "But Provis has forbidden him to have any more," David added with a chuckle. It was all very male, all very pally. And, of course, very colonial.

Part of the problem may have been that Francois was used to working for a bachelor. In Rhodesia, I remembered being told, servants frequently resented the appearance of a woman on the scene. But there was more to it than that. Although I'd grown up with servants, I had no idea how to treat them as an employer, particularly here in an independent country. As children we'd taken them for granted, flinging our dirty clothes on the floor to be washed, and assuming the servants would tidy up after us. Although we'd been taught to be polite and courteous towards them, my brother and I had been automatically autocratic. Once, arriving home from boarding school a day earlier than expected, my brother had ordered a stranger at the station to carry his suitcase the four and a half miles to our house. The first my mother knew of his arrival was the sight of her son striding up the drive with a black man behind him carrying a box on his head. It wasn't just our upbringing, it was our era.

My mother, who'd been a memsahib in India, had been more enlightened than most of her Rhodesian counterparts, but she'd still been essentially paternalistic. "Slave!" she'd exclaimed when a new gardener told her his name. "I can't possibly call you that," and promptly renamed him Job because he had a sad face. She'd shaken her head disapprovingly when the houseboy, Joseph, chose to spend his first pay packet on a cork helmet to keep the sun off his head rather than saving up for a bicycle. "What does he think God gave him woolly hair for?" she'd lamented.

So, although I'd thought about race, I hadn't really thought about the

41

manner of treating servants until I'd gone to England where there'd been a social revolution, and the working classes were no longer prepared to be subservient. I had come out to the Congo determined to change the outmoded attitudes I'd grown up with. I was going to treat my servant as my equal, as a friend as well as an employee. That, as any colonial could have told me, was a mistake. As far as Francois was now concerned, he felt free to be overfamiliar. He called me "tu" instead of the more respectful "vous". Though why shouldn't he? I asked myself. The Belgians, even before Independence, had been less formal than the British with their servants. Determined not to patronise Francois, I didn't offer him leftovers – not that there was much to give – or lock up the provisions. When food went missing I held my tongue. His need, I argued, was far greater than mine.

The truth was, however, that I felt uneasy at his familiarity. I cringed at his exaggerated chivalry, particularly when he handed me a tatty canna lily, picked no doubt from the garden, with the words, "un petit cadeau pour toi". At the same time, though, I didn't want to play the "madam" and boss him about or patronise him. I was trapped in the white man's guilt, trying to reconcile my so-called principles with the way of life I found myself in. It gave Francois the upper hand.

Although my fellow expats were only too happy to adopt colonial traditions, dressing their servants up in uniforms and ringing little bells at mealtimes, I didn't want to be like that. I was in a muddle. At the same time as trying to live by my own set of precepts, I was doing my best to fit in, and to be a good wife and mother. By nature untidy and dreamy, I wasn't much of a housewife. I knew that I was going to have to take my turn in entertaining the Dutch women, and I was dreading it. I had no idea how I was going to provide the obligatory mid-game coffee and cakes. And as the time approached, I began to panic. Finally, not to be outdone, I decided to splash out on some cakes from Le Petit Pâtisserie.

I could probably have asked for George to come and take me, but it wasn't my shopping day, and besides, part of me couldn't help feeling ashamed. There was something slightly obscene about swanning through Léopoldville in a company car with a black driver, let alone buying outrageously priced cakes. So I set off alone, pushing Charles in his pram. The pâtisserie, however, was further than I'd realised, and the day was hot. Charles, who'd just had his first birthday, became more and more restless. He insisted on walking. Heaving him in and out of his pram, and having to slow down to his pace, meant that it took forever to get there.

The shop was as mouth-watering as I remembered. Little almond biscuits, pies topped with fruit, pastries, luscious slices of thickly iced chocolate cake. I lingered, drooling, unable to make up my mind, while at the same time feeling guilty. Then, careless of the price – I was not going to be outdone by the Dutch – I chose some éclairs stuffed with cream. The shop packed them carefully into a cardboard box, even wrapping tissue paper round each one; I put the éclairs and Charles into the pram, and we set off home. Francois had left by the time we got back to the house. Charles, who'd not been given the option of walking, was fractious. I put the éclairs straight into the fridge in case the cream went off and then fed Charles and put him into his bath.

It wasn't just the mid-game refreshment I'd been worried about, it was also my house with its hideous furniture and ugly curtains. When the dainty Dutch ladies arrived to play bridge the next day, I was painfully aware of the lack of what my mother would have called "standards". I couldn't even manage my "boy". During the game, Francois kept putting his head through the door and signalling to me. I ignored him, as I had already explained what he had to do. After the first rubber, I went briefly into the kitchen to tell him to bring in the coffee. I didn't linger because I had to get back to my guests. Francois arrived with a tray laden with the wedding-present silver and the bone china we'd had shipped out to the Congo – there, at least, I wasn't letting my mother down. But there were no cakes.

"Could you bring in the cakes?" I said, trying to sound both authoritative and calm.

"Madame . . ."

"Now."

He arrived with the éclairs, still in their box. I opened it up. Inside, there was a soggy mess of cream and pastry, mixed up with tissue paper. Charles must have squashed them in his pram. I shut the box before anyone could see anything. They were too expensive to simply throw away. Taking them into the kitchen, I asked Francois to take off the paper and put them on a plate. No one said anything when he handed them round, but I felt for Francois, as well as for myself. At one stage in the game, someone made the joke about fine eyes being better than finesse.

I had always turned my nose up at colonial "standards" and despised my mother for adhering to them, but it was difficult, if not impossible, to cut myself off from the society I was living in. I couldn't help wondering how Mrs Roux, with her feminist as well as racial absolutes, would have dealt with my situation. When I'd met up with her in Johannesburg, I'd been aware of letting her down; of not turning out to be the sort of person she'd hoped for. Just as she was leaving, she'd said: "One of the things I can never understand is how you girls always have the right clothes to wear for every occasion."

In fact, I was not in the slightest like that, but one of the more down-to-earth problems of having to stay passport-less in Johannesburg had been the climate. It had been midwinter in South Africa, and I had just come from Iran, where it was summer. The Congo, as everyone knew, was permanently hot. And so the only thing I'd had to wear that was remotely warm enough was a pink suit I'd brought with me because it was the only item of smart clothing I possessed. I knew that I'd betrayed my maths teacher's ideals by leaving South Africa and not following the academic career she'd had in mind for me, but her words "you girls" – lumping me with the spoilt rich girls from school – had felt like a final indictment.

I was too young to realise that it may well have been a sign of her feelings of inadequacy. Instead, I agonised about the sort of person I was, and what I ought to be. And although part of me felt that I should have been able to rise above the dreariness of our Léopoldville house – after all, what were material possessions? – another part of me yearned for domesticity. I desperately wanted to build a nest; to make my house pretty; to make it my own.

It wasn't only the government furniture and concrete floors of the house we'd been assigned that depressed me. The block of flats behind cast both the house and garden into permanent gloom. The light in the Congo was nothing like the sparkling, clear skies of Rhodesia or South Africa. Even when there wasn't a tropical downpour, the permanent fug of heat produced a haze that blotted out the blue. And there weren't even lush tropical plants in our garden to make up for it. The ground was sandy, presumably part of the old riverbed, and, apart from the mango tree beside the house, the only things that grew were a few canna lilies and a lawn as sparse as a balding head. What's more, it was impossible to buy anything locally, not even ethnic fabrics. The old hands knew to bring all their carpets and curtains, as well as their knick-knacks, with them. That was something Mr Clayton hadn't told us about.

"Your husband should complain," Mrs Van Royan said when I confided in her. She was a strong woman who, without making a song and dance, tended to get what she wanted. Her flat was beautifully furnished with simple, elegant fittings.

"He'd never do that . . ."

"Oh, my husband does not like to do these things either," she went on, noticing my expression, "he is too soft. But you must insist."

Insist. How could I insist? David may have joined a new male fraternity, but he was not by nature a pushy man. I knew that he was unsure of himself, and he needed me to be supportive. Besides, insisting went against everything I'd been taught. We women were supposed to be the conciliators, and not make trouble. Men had to be treated with kid gloves in case they lost confidence. They needed to believe that they were the dominant partner. My mother, who was the strong one in the family, had fostered the illusion by treating my father as lord and master. I, on the other hand, genuinely believed that women should have their own jobs and be people in their own right. Alone, and with nobody much to talk to, I was having difficulty squaring the circle.

Chapter 5

"The newly independent Congo," I dictated into a borrowed tape recorder – I was sitting under the dining-room table draped in a blanket to simulate a studio and muffle any exterior sounds – "is like a chrysalis. The butterfly has yet to emerge . . ." I'd sent a piece off to the BBC, telling them that I had access to a tape recorder and that I would be able to read my reports beautifully as I had once been an actress. To my amazement, they replied, sending me a tape though politely imploring me: "Please try not to sound like an actress."

"The butterfly has yet to emerge"? What butterfly, for God's sake? *Woman's Hour* had probably taken the piece because I'd told the English listeners about practical things like the price of beans, as well as trying to explain what it felt like as a woman, living in this quagmire. The truth was, I had absolutely no idea what was really happening out there in the jungle. I was still trying to make some sort of sense of my own discombobulated life.

Soon after arriving, I'd decided to take a walk to the river. I not only wanted to get out of the house, I wanted to get a feeling of tropical Africa. My brief glimpse from the air as we landed had, surprisingly, been of flat savannah grassland. I knew it wasn't all like that. I believed that if only I could get a whiff of the world beyond the confines of the house and the dreary suburbs, I would be able to get some sense of the real Congo. I had a vision of that huge, wild river winding up into the interior and curling its tail round, like a snake. It had been one of the last places on earth to be discovered and mapped by Europeans, and that idea had fired my imagination. I thought of the early explorers, like Henry Morton Stanley, hacking their way through virgin forest; of monkeys swinging on ropes and creatures prowling through the undergrowth. I dreamed of the romance of the celluloid Congo: of *The African Queen*; of Humphrey Bogart chugging down-river on a steamer with his missionary companion; of Katharine Hepburn waking up the next morning, a woman transformed by sex, and diffidently addressing her rough-hewn lover as "dear".

It was hot pushing a pram along the streets. The only evidence of jungle was the ubiquitous palm trees, which weren't, as I'd already discovered, the tall, elegant kind that you see in picture postcards beside idyllic sandy beaches. They were short and squat, and carried bunches of hard yellow nuts at the top of their trunks. It was from these that the palm oil was extracted. I remembered a jingle that I'd heard over and over again on Lourenço Marques radio when I was at school:

Use Palmolive soap,
Use Palmolive soap,
And see how your complexion improves.
Palmolive soap is the quality soap
And that is your best guarantee, tra la . . .

I found myself humming it, then stopped, feeling a nasty taste in my mouth. It brought back the empty materialism of white South Africa.

It was a long way to the river along the sandy, rutted, ill-kept roads, but we got there eventually. There were no romantic vistas, just huge metal containers on the beach. Inside each of them were thousands and thousands of gallons of palm oil, squeezed, crushed from those little nuts I'd seen along the way. They'd been harvested from plantations up-river and brought down in oil tankers. They formed the basis of all the soap products. Just as the Texan wells had benefited American millionaires in the 1920s, the golden palm oil had made the Company's fortune. Looking at the metal containers, I was struck by the fact that in their quest for wealth, people invariably trashed the countryside it came from.

I stood there, peering past the oil tankers at the sluggish, dirty river and tried to imagine those wild stretches upcountry; the romance of the unspoilt jungle; a people uncontaminated by us and what we stood for. Instead, the wretched jingle kept playing itself compulsively through my brain:

Use Palmolive soap,
Use Palmolive soap,
And see how your complexion improves.

Pictures I'd seen in newspapers and magazines when I was at school flashed through my head; typical Fifties drawings of jolly black ladies in doeks exclaiming with delight over a packet of soap powder that got their clothes whiter than white, as if that was all they'd ever wanted or aspired to. Even in apartheid South Africa, especially in apartheid South Africa, companies were targeting the people least able to afford their products. People they presumed wanted to emulate the white people who had all the power. The irony was that here in the newly independent Congo, the people were so poor they weren't even worth targeting. That was presumably why soap powder was one of the many things it was impossible to get. Their main agricultural resource was exported, as it always had been, to make rich countries richer.

I was reminded of Victorian times when Conrad wrote his *Heart of*

49

Darkness. During the land-grab in Africa in the nineteenth century, it had been insignificant little Belgium that had ended up with this apparently godforsaken piece of Africa. The British Empire already owned large chunks of the world, and had shown no particular interest when Henry Morton Stanley told them of his discoveries. So it had been the Belgian King Léopold who had funded the explorer and claimed this vast, unknown tract of land Europeans called terra incognita as his own private kingdom. He'd been in luck. As well as the hugely valuable minerals in the eastern Congo, he had discovered rubber trees and the palm trees with their precious nuts.

The sheer scale of this virgin territory partly explains the monstrous nature of King Léopold's greed. The more he got, the more he wanted. The indigenous Congolese had been rounded up, forcibly employed, and driven like animals in order to increase the productivity of his newly seized land. If they fell short on their quotas they were beaten, brutalised, and had their hands chopped off – a singularly stupid and inappropriate punishment. The cruelty had been so unspeakable, it was almost impossible to read about, much less contemplate.

"It's not like that now," David had said when I'd argued that we were still exploiting Congolese people. "Modern employment methods are fair and humane. Besides, they need us. They need the Company in order to bring the people prosperity."

"But we're reaping the profits."

"They're reaping them as well. And we'll hand over as soon as they're ready. The Company has a policy of Africanisation, and as soon as there's a black man capable of doing the job, he'll get it."

He went on to explain how the Company was importing men from other countries like Ghana because very few of the indigenous Congolese were educated enough. This was because in the Fifties the Belgian government had installed a system where they had educated a so-called elite whom they called évolués – people who were presumably considered to have "evolved". This system was, however, limited to primary school education. The only secondary schooling was through the Catholic Church, which ran seminaries to train Congolese men to become priests. Although a university had been set up at the end of the Fifties, there had only been one graduate by the time the Congo was given its independence. That was the reason, David explained, why the Company had to import white managers, just as they had before Independence.

David may have been right, but as I witnessed every time I went to the club, as far as those white managers were concerned, nothing had changed. They still assumed an automatic superiority. They didn't care a damn what happened to black people. Nor, for that matter, what happened to the country as a whole – provided it didn't affect them too much. As far as they were concerned, the mess was all the Congolese people's fault for demanding independence in the first place.

"They know better now," the old hands in the club would smugly argue whenever the subject of independence came up. "Most of them wish we were back in power." It was what everyone said. What they believed. When everything had got sufficiently chaotic, the Congolese government would come back to the West, cap in hand, and say, "We were wrong. Please, come back." And as far as the Congolese people themselves were concerned – those who didn't have enough to eat and who had witnessed the chaos into which their country had fallen – they may have had a point. But that didn't alter the fact that the Congolese had the basic right to determine their own future.

"Since Independence, everything is pot à pot," George told me on one of our shopping expeditions. "Pot à pot" was the slang for mud and mess.

"Why?"

"It is because of the death of our leader, Patrice Lumumba."

"Really?"

"They should not have murdered him."

"Who were they?"

"We do not know." Even George had the capacity to clam up, so I didn't press him.

When I had read about the murder of Patrice Lumumba in England I hadn't taken too much notice. He was one of those people the British press had loved to hate. A humble post office clerk who'd become an évolué – though I hadn't known the term in those days. As a beer salesman he'd been imprisoned for embezzlement, which he claimed to be politically motivated, and then spent a second term in jail for inciting unrest. As far as the British press was concerned, he'd rocketed to eminence with nothing more than his charisma to offer. The most damning thing about him, however, had been the fact that he was a dreaded "Commie". He had co-founded a political party called the MNC – Mouvement National Congolais – and at the Independence Day celebrations he'd denounced the Belgian regime and its past history in the Congo. This had, not surprisingly, incensed the Belgians as well as their king. Lumumba had then gone on to cosy up to the Soviets, finally accepting a consignment of military equipment from the USSR. As far as the press was concerned, he'd been a troublemaker. His death, from the perspective of faraway Europe, had seemed like a stroke of good fortune.

George, however, was forcing me to think again. To him, Patrice Lumumba was a hero. In 1960, when he'd been voted in as prime minister, he'd formed a government with Joseph Kasavubu as president. But, although the people had been given autonomy in theory, the army had been kept under the control of the Belgians. This meant that the newly formed government had soon got into trouble when the privates rebelled against their Belgian officers. Lumumba, who had appointed Mobutu as his private secretary, promoted him to Chief of Staff of the army to deal with the insurrection. Although Mobutu had managed to persuade the soldiers to return to their barracks, he was – or so he claimed – unable to do anything about Lumumba's other headache, breakaway Katanga. The United Nations were equally ineffectual and so, in desperation, Lumumba had turned to the Soviet Union for help.

As a European, I couldn't help seeing why Lumumba's political affiliation had troubled the West. When I'd first come to England, I'd been sceptical about the generally felt "Reds-under-the-beds" paranoia. Many of the white South Africans fighting against apartheid, including Mrs Roux, were members of the Communist party. But then, they hadn't had to deal directly with the Russian threat and the Cold War. This threat had seemed very real that cold, cold Christmas just before David had walked into the flat and made his announcement about going to the Congo. Russian warships had been spotted carrying nuclear missiles to Cuba, and the new President Kennedy had had to call their bluff. Either they withdrew their ships, he told the USSR in an ultimatum, or he would give orders to press the nuclear button. For the few days before Russia withdrew, we'd faced what had genuinely seemed to be the prospect of annihilation.

When I'd first arrived in England in 1956 I'd assumed that all British people would be outraged at the South African system of apartheid. In fact, most of the ones I met were either ignorant or indifferent. "Why don't you stand on a soapbox?" one society hostess had said waspishly when I'd aired my anti-apartheid views. It wasn't done, she strongly implied, to spout about that sort of thing in English drawing rooms. So I'd tended not to talk about it. African politics became less pressing, less urgent. And, in a way, it had been a relief not to have to worry about race.

David was a conservative. And although he had no in-built prejudice, it wasn't a subject to which he'd given much thought. His views on the economy and the state of world affairs were rational and well argued, and I'd tended to accept his explanation of things.

Returning to Africa, however, had brought the whole question right back into my consciousness. With his very English upbringing, it was hardly surprising that David was ignorant about the subtleties of race issues, but I had lived in Africa. I'd seen attitudes harden. It was one of the reasons why I found it so valuable talking to George. It gave me a chance to try and understand the other side.

"What do the people think of President Adoula?" I asked him during one of our expeditions.

"They do not like him."

"Why?"

George looked embarrassed.

"I do not know."

A barrier had come down. A gate closed. And I was on the other side.

Chapter 6

Thinking about it, it was hardly surprising that the Congolese people should mistrust a president who had been foisted on them by the West, particularly in view of the food shortages. Despite the presence of UN troops, the most sinister aspect of the stagnant pool in which we'd found ourselves was the apparent lack of any law and order. It was something I tried to avoid thinking about. Even though, as David had cheerfully told us on our journey from the airport to Léopoldville, there were bandits out there in the darkness, I needed to leave them "out there". Just as I had always counted on the fact that there would be enough to eat, so, up till now, I had assumed that, if the worst came to the worst, someone in authority would look after my welfare. But there was a part of me that knew I was deluding myself. Not only was there little evidence of a butterfly emerging from its chrysalis, the only certainty appeared to be anarchy.

David seemed unconcerned at the situation. Both he and the ever-cheerful Thoby, who came round most evenings, made a joke of it all. Thoby positively revelled in horror stories. He told us how some thieves had managed, in broad daylight, to remove all four tyres of a Volkswagen parked on the edge of the boulevard in the middle of town. "When the owner got back he found it sitting beside the pavement like a legless duck, ha, ha." The police – the Force Publique – he declared, were worse than useless, they were a positive menace. One of them had stopped a car because the child inside had been waving a water pistol out of the window. Even though the pistol had turned out to be a toy, the policeman had taken it into his head that he was being insulted. The father, who was white, had been arrested and spent the night in jail. I knew Thoby loved exaggerating, and his stories were so outrageous that I only half believed them. I couldn't really imagine a black man having the nerve to put a white man into jail.

Then, one morning, while I was working on my typewriter, I heard raised voices outside. I sauntered to the back door and froze. Charles was playing as usual in the sand. On the other side of the fence a young man in a soldier's uniform was waving a gun at him. I wanted not to believe what I was seeing. The scene was so surreal it had to be a game. At the same time, I knew it was deadly serious.

Up till then I had barely spoken to the gardener, Eugène. Now it dawned on me with a clarity induced by the deluge of adrenalin flooding my body that my child's life was in his hands. The youth in the soldier's uniform looked so crazy that part of me reckoned that even if he did fire the gun he would miss. It was the sort of thing that happened in the movies. Eugène appeared to be reasoning with him and I stayed still. I knew, with the razor-sharp awareness that comes with crises, that if I dashed out into the garden and snatched my child up into my arms, he really would shoot. I was torn between rationality and maternal instinct. I felt like a coward for staying still and watching, and yet I knew that I was impotent.

With the rational part of my brain, the part that was furiously calculating what I would do under various circumstances, I noticed that, even though the gun-toting maniac was shouting at him, Eugène was talking in a quiet voice. It gave me hope that someone, even if it wasn't I, was in charge. The scene probably didn't go on for more than a few seconds, a minute or two at most, but it felt like forever. At last the soldier lowered his gun. He looked sulky. There was a bit more dialogue and then, reluctantly, he turned and, trying to look casual, he sauntered off.

"What happened?" I asked Francois, who had been watching the whole scene and was now discussing it with the gardener in Lingala. I had, by this time, dashed over to Charles and picked him up. I was clinging to my child, shaking with shock.

"The child was throwing pebbles over the fence," Francois explained, "and the soldier, who was passing by, thought they were aimed at him."

Eugène had, I was told, been trying to get across to him that a one-year-old child couldn't possibly have known what he was doing, that he would never have deliberately thrown stones in order to harm anybody. The soldier had insisted that he had been insulted.

I looked at my gardener and realised I hadn't even bothered to get to know him properly, even though he played with my son every day. He was a young man, tall and gentle-looking. The shaking had turned into sobs of relief.

When I told David about what had happened, he pooh-poohed the idea that the soldier would actually have shot Charles. "He was just showing off," he said. "They've got to flex their muscles to show us that they're nominally in charge, but it doesn't really mean anything." David sounded not only like the rational, well-educated Englishman he was, but also like the other men at the club.

"Probably wasn't even a soldier," Thoby said when we told him the story later that evening. "Most of them don't get paid, so they sell off their uniforms to the highest bidder." I was half aware of being treated like a child, the little woman who'd had a shock and needed to be protected. Both David and Thoby laughed, and I realised that my story had been put into the same league as that of the father whose son had been aiming a water pistol out of the car window. It would do the rounds.

Although I felt confused and subliminally angry, I couldn't rationalise it. What could I have said? No one knew what was really happening "out there". And anyway, I told myself, how did I know they weren't right? No harm had been done. No one had shot my baby. Humans, I believed, were by and large good and rational beings. I clung to that thought. And yet, part of me knew that there was a universal madness going on.

"You know, the Africans are the only people on earth that never invented the wheel," Thoby remarked, adding, "that's why they can't run this country."

It was exactly the sort of thing the Rhodesians had said. "You can't trust a kaffir . . . It'll take hundreds of years of civilisation . . . never in my lifetime . . ." Even my father had echoed those sentiments. "Give me one good British workman and he's worth half a dozen natives." It was as if he'd been sucked into the mindset of the country we'd immigrated to.

That evening Thoby told us about Rwanda-Burundi, and the fabled Mountains of the Moon situated on the eastern border. "There are two tribes, the Tutsis and the Hutus." He exaggerated the "oo" in order to make them sound funny, like an Edward Lear limerick. "The Tutsis are tall and beautiful and the Hutus are short and ugly. Naturally, it's the Tutsis who are the aristocrats, and up till now they've been the top dogs. But the Hutus have decided that they've had enough, so they've taken it into their woolly little heads to cut off the legs of the Tutsis – to make them the same size . . . ha, ha . . ."

Ha. Ha. Thoby's story had summoned up a picture of Babar the Elephant facing an unknown tribe of fuzzy-wuzzies. The amputated legs made me think of the horror that had been the Congo in the days of King Léopold. Black, bloody, disenfranchised limbs began to invade my dreams. Why did these things happen? First of all we cut off their hands, and then they cut off each other's legs. Just the thought made me feel physically sick. And yet, in another way, I too was learning to be immune. In telling the story of the gunman threatening to shoot Charles, I had managed to sanitise it, to make it seem less awful; as if the whole thing had happened to someone else.

Even so, I couldn't go on turning a completely blind eye to what was happening. The pot à pot, the turmoil of "out there", had not only threatened to enter my garden, it had insinuated itself into my consciousness. Whatever his mental state, the soldier was presumably employed by the government. They were supposed to be in charge and looking after people like me. I was also wrestling with the past. I found myself becoming obsessed with what had taken place after Independence; les événements de soixante, as they were called; the events of Sixty. I knew that the soldiers had revolted against their Belgian officers and had gone on to commit atrocities. But nobody ever said what those atrocities were. No one who was actually there wanted to talk about it. It was almost as if they were, in some obscure way, ashamed of what had happened to them then. At the same time, les événements de soixante had become mythologised. "At Independence they thought they'd wake up the next day with white faces," Thoby joked, even though he hadn't been there. The whole phenomenon had become a myth.

And then I overheard a fragment of conversation in the club. Two Belgian women were talking to one another. "She can't stop sticking pins into herself," the one said as if it were a perfectly normal thing to do. But the idea of a young woman compulsively sticking pins into herself became lodged in my imagination. Soldiers hadn't just waved guns at children; during les événements de soixante they had come into people's houses and committed their atrocities.

No one had mentioned the word rape, but I was swamped by an indefinable apprehension.

Chapter 7

One of the rules of my upbringing had been that it was a sin to brood. Introspection was selfindulgent. Complaining was bad form. And there was no point in agonising about things you could do nothing about. One should always, my mother had banged into us, make the most of things as they were and not make a fuss.

"Just think of what it's like in England now and be thankful," my new friend Diana said tartly to the nanny she'd brought out with her from England when she complained of the Congolese heat. We were sitting beside a little pool, artfully tucked into the landscape with water cascading down the boulders. I agreed with Diana. We had been brought up with the same rules. Who could complain when they had their own ready-made swimming pool?

I'd met Diana at the British Council play-reading group. Her husband was high up in the hierarchy of the British Embassy. They lived out of town and to my delight and gratification, she had asked me to tea. Her house was built on the slope of a rocky hill, where the plateau of the interior started to tumble towards the coast. After the stultifying suburbs of Léopoldville, it felt blissfully cool because it was exposed to the wind, and there was an open view over the countryside.

I admired Diana. She was a no-nonsense sort of person. She was also extraordinarily beautiful. With her long golden hair drawn back in the style of the Pre-Raphaelites and tied in a loose knot behind her head, she looked like a goddess. More importantly, being used to going abroad, she knew how to cope. The reason she had brought her nanny with her was that she had several children, including a little boy the same age as Charles. But as well as admiring Diana, I was also a bit daunted.

When we'd first arrived in Léopoldville I'd made a point of going to the Embassy and signing the visitor's book. This, I'd been told, would ensure an invitation to the Queen's Birthday Party. In fact, I needn't have bothered. The party wasn't exclusive at all. All the British expats, as far as I could see, were invited. We, however, were to go with my new friend Diana and her husband. That gave us an automatic cachet.

Diana was well aware of her position. She swept into the British Embassy like royalty, with us in tow. When we got to the doorway of the main drawing room she suddenly froze. This had probably been thought out beforehand – Diana, an enthusiastic thespian, had been cast as Titania in the forthcoming British Council production of *A Midsummer Night's Dream*. Having made sure that everyone was aware of who was being snubbed, she then swept on, head held high, into the drawing room.

The object of the cut was Janette Jones. She was, as everyone knew, a "fallen woman". And to be fair to Diana, "living in sin" was in those days generally considered beyond the pale. But this was a particularly juicy scandal. Bob Jones, the lover, worked for the Company. He was a Company engineer, and on his previous tour of duty in Léopoldville he had apparently met and fallen in love with Janette, a married woman. What made the snub particularly meaningful was that Janette had previously been married to someone working in the British Embassy.

It should have been a romantic story, except that neither Bob nor Janette quite looked the part. He was middle-aged, portly, and going bald; she was rather insipid-looking. She was, however, at least ten years younger than Bob, which was presumably her allure. It was more difficult to work out what she'd seen in him. Whatever it was, it must have

61

been pretty electric because, when they went back to England on leave, Janette changed her name by deed poll – divorces were harder to come by in those days – and, abandoning her children, returned to the Congo as Bob's "wife".

I'd frequently seen the Joneses at the club, but had never really talked to either of them. Diana's public snub whetted my appetite. Although I could not imagine leaving my child under any circumstances, part of me couldn't help admiring Janette. It must have taken a lot of guts to invite the opprobrium of people like Diana. I decided that there had to be hidden coals smouldering in her rather ordinary-looking exterior – coals which the improbable Bob had surely ignited. So, although I didn't imagine we'd have much in common, I decided to try to get myself invited to tea.

It was the conundrum of the children that fascinated me. Bob was no Vronsky, Janette no Anna Karenina. Despite the fact that her husband had been deemed legally to be the innocent party and given custody, I still couldn't understand how she could have abandoned her children in England, or, indeed, what led her into the arms of another.

The Joneses lived not far from us, but because Bob had a higher position in the Company, theirs was a more prestigious bungalow with a large garden. There was a swing and a seesaw, and the garden paraphernalia enabled me to ask about her children. She told me their ages and sexes, and I would dearly have liked to imagine her eyes turning misty, but she was not going to give me the satisfaction by manifesting any emotion. Nor was she forthcoming about her relationship with Bob, though that was a more difficult subject to broach. I did my best, but it required a huge leap of the imagination to see her as a femme fatale.

While we were having tea, Bob came back from the office. That merely deepened the mystery. Bob was a blunt, down-to-earth Northerner. I simply couldn't imagine what sex appeal he might have. He liked his tea strong, he said, sitting out on the lawn, tipping the pot backwards and forwards in order to blacken the brew. Janette was more like milk and water. Then he shouted at the "boy" to make a fresh pot. But the thing that really disconcerted me was the way he treated Janette. She may have been one up from the "boy", but she was still a mere woman. When Bob wanted something, he didn't ask, he ordered, and he didn't look at his "wife" when addressing her. They might have been married for ever. Fortunately, he didn't take too much notice of me, and later that afternoon, to my relief, David joined us.

As the evening progressed, I found myself disliking Bob more and more. He behaved as if he owned Janette.

"She goes to the hairdresser every week," he said proudly – I hadn't even realised that there was a hairdresser in Léopoldville – "she likes to keep smart. To look after herself."

Janette's hair was, I realised, her most striking feature. She normally wore it up, but I had also seen it flowing free. It was long and wavy, and all I could conclude was that she had been his fairy-tale princess, his Rapunzel. I pictured her standing at her window, letting down her hair and yearning for love. Any love.

Later that evening, eavesdropping on what I imagined was supposed to be a boys-only conversation, I heard Bob describe some woman as "so old you could put your foot in it". Up till then, I'd had no idea that some men felt that way about women. I wondered how old you had to get before men could put their foot in it. Would David be saying the same thing about me in a few years' time? And what about men? Didn't they also have a duty to keep themselves up to scratch? Did Bob imagine his considerable beer belly added to his personal allure? And if this was the way he treated the love of his life, what about the real Mrs Jones back in Bolton, or wherever it was she came from? I pictured her as a mouse, sitting out in this very garden on a deck chair, knowing her place, only to have it usurped by a younger woman.

And yet, the fact that Janette's only attraction appeared to be her comparative youth made me feel sympathetic towards her. I'd imagined a cold, unemotional Englishman as her erstwhile diplomatic husband, "dead from the neck down", as they said. Perhaps Bob had provided a great big shoulder to cry on. Perhaps, I speculated, her husband had been a secret wife-beater. It hadn't occurred to me that it might have been Bob who was the beater; that she yearned for something meatier, a stronger brew than an academic diplomat. Perhaps she needed Bob's mixture of fantasy and chauvinism. But I couldn't help wondering what would happen to her if Bob got tired of her. Or, indeed, how Janette would cope when her prince – as he surely would – turned back into a frog.

David, thankfully, wasn't at all like Bob. He was more like the gentle Mr Van Royan. We dined with the Van Royans from time to time and, when there were no other guests, we played bridge. Although I didn't come from a card-playing family, I'd learned the game when I got to know David. To my surprise, I discovered that I enjoyed it. I not only liked the mental challenge, but discovered I had an unexpected taste for risk. David and I made a good partnership. He played the cards impeccably, while I was the intuitive one. I would jump him into impossibly high bids, and he would make the contract. We trusted one another.

Bridge also gave me the opportunity to study the individuals we played with. I'd come to the conclusion that when people were absorbed in the game, they no longer projected the person they wanted the world to see, but instead revealed their true selves. Our bridge sessions allowed me to study the bond between the Van Royans. Physically, they could not have been more different. While she was big and motherly, he was delicate, with an ascetic Nordic face. Watching the way they sorted their cards and listened to one another's bids, deciding on which one would play, I became more and more aware of how much they depended on one another.

They'd been living in Jakarta in Indonesia when the Second World War started. They'd both been in their early twenties, and Mr Van Royan had, even in those days, been employed by the Company. When the Japanese invaded the country, they'd been taken away to separate concentration camps. The two young children had gone with their mother. And, although Mrs Van Royan had had to endure the anxiety of caring for her children, at least she'd had their company. Mr Van Royan had been by himself. He never mentioned the war. She, on the other hand, frequently talked about it when we were alone together.

Predictably, it was a horrendous story. Mrs Van Royan had had to virtually starve herself to ensure a minimum of food for her children, and even then one of them had got seriously ill and almost died. Sabine, the older one, had survived psychologically, she told me, but Wilhelm, the younger, still suffered from chronic depression. The parents had not seen each other or had any communication until Japan capitulated and peace was declared five years later. As I watched them sort their cards, it struck me that it was the shared horror as well as their love for one another which had brought them so close together.

With the war over and normality restored, they had gone on to have another child. Both of them were a good deal older by this time, and their daughter was consequently very precious. They'd called her Clara, the beloved one, and even though she was eleven years old and the Company paid staff boarding-school fees, they couldn't bear to let her go. She had finished her primary schooling, which meant that, on the days Mrs Van Royan didn't play bridge, she had to give her daughter lessons.

The Van Royans had been much the same age as David and me when they were captured. I had read books about the Japanese torture camps and the sadistic punishments they'd meted out to prisoners, but I'd always assumed that the prisoners were soldiers. It had never occurred to me that civilians had been involved as well. And although I found the story fascinating and the subsequent solidarity of their relationship comforting, I was disturbed by the notion that ordinary businesspeople could get caught up like that in a war.

These apprehensions were not the sort of things I could or would have discussed with David. We had both grown up during the Second World War. While Mr and Mrs Van Royan had been prisoners in Indonesia, I'd been living in India and David in England. There was no doubt that, although neither of us had had a hard time, the experience had affected the way we looked at life. I'd avidly gobbled up war stories, while at the same time believing that that sort of thing would never happen again. I'd needed to take an upbeat view of the past to have faith in the future.

And yet I couldn't disregard the ever-present food shortages. One night after Francois had gone home, I emptied onto the floor a bag of rice I'd managed to get hold of, as I'd discovered some weevils in it. Then David and I got down onto our hands and knees and, spreading out a handful at a time, we painstakingly sifted every grain. David had protested when I'd first suggested it, but I insisted.

"It's Charles," I said, "he needs a variety of foods. We can't just feed him on tins. And we can always wash it before we cook it."

It took hours picking out every single one of those disgusting little black creatures. And even when we'd finished, we were aware that we'd almost certainly missed some of them. Not to mention the invisible eggs. I knew that they would hatch and breed again, infesting the rest of the rice. I also knew that at some level David found the whole operation profoundly demeaning. It wasn't just getting down on his hands and knees. He felt that as a man he was supposed to be the provider.

Chapter 8

So food continued to be a permanent worry. It wasn't simply a matter of barter. For the Belgians, it was a kind of game. They had a word for it: débrouillard, which literally meant "de-fogged". It was the highest compliment one could pay a person. It meant that you were smart and could get one over on someone else. In this new country, ruthless inventiveness was considered a virtue. Greed was a game. And everyone was on to it.

I'd met other women besides Diana whose husbands were working for the British Embassy, and I'd discovered that even some of the most innocent-seeming wives were débrouillard. They had diplomatic immunity, and they used it. The Embassy had a shop, a sort of Naafi where the staff could buy imported goods, including alcohol, at the official rate of exchange, which made it ludicrously cheap. They could also take a boat over to Brazzaville on the other side of the river for shopping expeditions. Brazzaville, or Brazza as it was known, was the capital of Congo-Brazzaville, a French colony. There were no troubles there, I'd been told, and there were plenty of luxury foods to be bought. As diplomats, the staff was allowed to change the Congolese francs for Brazza francs at the official rate of exchange. Then, when they got back to Léopoldville, they could sell unspent Brazza francs on the black market for ten times their official value. That way, if they were clever, they ended up richer than when they'd started out.

And it wasn't just the Belgians and the British; everyone cheated. The

United Nations personnel had taken the currency fiddling to an even higher level. They were able to buy much-needed goods like cars and bicycles and sewing machines from overseas with Congolese francs at the official rate of exchange. They then sold the stuff on the black market and changed the Congolese francs back into hard currency at the official rate. It was no wonder that those in high positions went back to their countries of origin as millionaires.

Not that we could preach. We also sold our hard currency on the black market. But that was as far as David would go. He was definitely not dé-brouillard. Nor was I, though I probably would have been, given the chance. We both suffered in silence while I, at any rate, boiled with inner resentment. But if I was feeling angry, how about the people on the street? We at least had the hard currency to sell. We also had our food hamper to look forward to, although having had to travel by ship all the way from England and then be put on a train at the port of Matadi, two hundred miles away, it took ages to get to us.

We'd been allotted a certain amount of money to spend and had chosen the provisions before leaving England, but as that had been several months before, neither of us had any idea what we'd ordered. When at long last it did arrive, however, we were euphoric. The hamper itself had been boxed in a wooden crate. Like children with a treat, we waited till Francois had gone home before levering off the planks. As we started to unpack, I had a flashback to the London flat and me singing "Bongo Bongo Bongo, I don't wanna leave the Congo". It seemed a very long time ago. "Don't want no bright lights, false teeth, doorbells" – though what false teeth and doorbells had to do with so-called civilisation, I couldn't imagine. But I'd had an equally false vision of the jungle that the singer had been so reluctant to leave. It had been the sort of jungle where solitary white men dined in dinner jackets.

Each item in our precious hamper was wrapped in a protective layer of paper. Little, expensive pots of shrimps, anchovies and artichoke hearts appeared as if by magic. There were two pots of Patum Peperium, anchovy paste that was spread on toast in gentlemen's clubs. Even some tins of cod's roe disguised as caviar emerged from the growing sea of paper. They were exciting, luxurious, delicious items, but as the piles grew, a weight started to settle on my heart. What we needed, what I realised I'd been hoping for, were some basics. Things like flour and salt and sugar. There was a pot of Oxford marmalade, which Thoby was later to appreciate, but some Marmite and baked beans wouldn't have gone amiss. And then, to our great joy and delight, a huge tin the size of a football appeared at the bottom. It was a whole Edam cheese. It must have been David's idea, as it was his favourite. It felt like a redemption.

By this stage we owed hospitality to several people, including Diana, so we decided to throw a wine-and-cheese party. I would make little eats with the shrimps and "caviar" on drop scones – we did actually have some flour at that stage, as well as the tinned milk and Sannie's eggs – and there was also the precious cheese. Hopefully, some of our more well-connected friends would bring wine. Apart from that, we would have to make do with local beer.

With the cheese as the centrepiece of our party, we waited till all our guests had arrived before the ceremonial opening of the Edam. David even started with a few words. The tin had a metal strip round its middle with its own key, like the tins of sardines at the time, and so, amid laughter and cheering, David slotted the key into the end of the metal strip and began to turn. First there was the hint of an unpleasant whiff. Then, as he went on, an evil-smelling liquid started seeping out. It began as a dribble, and then gushed onto the floor. Some anaerobic creature must have got into it and had a field day. David was left holding a messy carcass with a lining of yellowy-green sludge.

This time it wasn't just the loss of face – and after all that certainly wasn't my fault – it was also the waste that upset me. To begin with, no one made a joke; the smell was too frightful for that. Our guests all moved away from the spot holding their noses and giggling politely while Francois was summoned with a bucket and mop. I imagined the smell penetrating their clothes. Mercifully, Thoby salvaged the situation with a quip about a "foul fiend in the football fraternity".

With the paucity of food, everyone went on to get thoroughly drunk. At some stage in the evening Charles, who had woken up and started to cry, joined the party. He was spotted staggering around in his nappy drinking the dregs from the beer glasses. He was also, it was claimed, saying "cheers".

"Well, I think that was a success," David said when everyone had gone and we were getting ready for bed.

"You can't be serious."

"Everyone seemed to be enjoying themselves."

"What about the cheese?"

"I don't think anyone minded."

But I minded. And it wasn't just the cheese. Towards the end of the evening Diana had come up to me and whispered: "I think you ought to know that there's a nappy in the loo." It was a dirty one. I'd changed Charles's nappy when he'd woken up and, as I usually did, dunked it in the lavatory before putting it to soak in the bucket. Only, this time it hadn't made it to the bucket. I pictured Diana lifting the disgusting thing out of the pan and then replacing it. It had been the final humiliation. I tried to tell myself that Diana had also had babies and that she had been through the whole procedure. But she also had nannies.

The real problem, though, was deeper. David was a loyal Company man but, apart from Thoby and the Van Royans, I hadn't invited any-one from the Company to our party. It was mainly snobbery, though I wouldn't have admitted that to David. The British class system was alive and well, even in the jungle. I simply couldn't have faced Janette letting her hair down, or, worse still, Bob holding forth on female allure. I knew that David was angry with me for not including his colleagues. But I was angry with his whole organisation. Most of the people working for the Company seemed to me pretty mediocre, and I felt that David was underappreciated.

Had we been able to articulate what we were really thinking, things might have been easier. But I knew that David saw any criticism of the Company as an implicit criticism of himself. His job was part of his sense of masculinity, and however carefully I trod, I felt I was permanently in danger of impugning it. We may have been compatible at the bridge table, but though he respected my intuition, and I in turn trusted his judgement as far as cards were concerned, we couldn't be as honest with each other in our day-to-day lives. We were ringed round with fences beyond which we both felt we couldn't go.

What I didn't admit was that I wasn't being honest with myself either. I didn't acknowledge my own feelings of growing despondency: with-out a car and dependent on lifts I felt trapped; I was also desperately lonely. I felt that I should be coping, and to admit that I wasn't meant giving in, and that would have meant losing too much face. Instead, I was trying to find a role for myself that I could live with.

"I hate Africa," a young painter had once said to me at a party. Like me, he had lived in another part of the continent.

"Then why are you here?" I asked him. He was single and, as far as I was aware, he wasn't making much money. His job didn't seem to dictate his location; he could have painted anywhere. There had to be a reason why he'd chosen the Congo to live and work in.

"Because I need to explore my soul," he declared. "I need to find out why I hate this bloody continent so much."

I hated Africa too, only I couldn't put my finger on a reason. Not a proper reason. I envied him; he knew what he was looking for, and could indulge his whims. The only worthwhile thing I felt I worried about was how to feed my baby. It seemed to me that everyone, except me, was somehow significant; that they were all living meaningful lives, except me.

To compensate for this sense of inadequacy, one of the roles I'd assigned myself was that of the brave-little-woman-who-makes-no-fuss. I'd noticed that the other wives seemed to have no compunction in taking even the most trivial ailments to the doctor. But I wasn't like that. I'd been brought up to bear pain and adversity and not seek medical advice unless it was absolutely essential. When, however, I had what I suspected was an early miscarriage, I succumbed. While I was at the clinic, I also mentioned that I had chronic diarrhoea. The doctor tested me for both, and when I went back to see him he told me that I had, indeed, been pregnant and that I had amoebic dysentery. I glanced at the lab report on his desk. The dysentery merited three exclamation marks. It was gratifying. At least I was medically significant.

It was probably the dysentery that had caused the miscarriage, and after swallowing a couple of gigantic brown capsules that looked like horse pills, I was duly cured. I then got pregnant again with what seems, in retrospect, astonishing haste and imprudence. That put me back on track. Now I had the expectant-mum to add to the brave-little-woman role. I needed to prove my worth – not only to the world, but above all to myself.

My real chance came on the tennis court. One of the things my South

73

African education had done was to teach me, in theory, how to play the game. But, although I may have looked good on the court, I had what I can only explain as a genetic flaw: my tennis racquet seldom made any effective contact with the ball. David insisted that it was in my mind, that all I had to do was keep my eye on the wretched thing and I would succeed. He may have been right. On the rare, very rare, occasions the technique I'd been taught at school worked, I would hit an ace. On one such occasion, stretching up for a perfect serve, I felt something in my tummy unzip. Again, the result was gratifyingly dramatic, not only on the tennis court, where my ball was unreturnable, but later at home as well. I started haemorrhaging in the middle of the night and had to be rushed to the clinic. The doctor put me on a table and, sticking a metal pipe-like contraption up inside me, cranked it open like a mediaeval torture instrument. Then, shining his torch, he peered up into the chasm of my vagina. David, meanwhile, looked on, impervious. No wonder, I thought, that women became "so old you could put your foot in it". I may as well have been a cow.

"You are very unlikely to keep this baby," the doctor told me, "so I would advise you not to take special care of yourself. You are young, you will conceive again. Go dancing."

Go dancing? Where did he imagine we were living?

The threatened miscarriage gave me an excuse to give up tennis, but otherwise I carried on as the doctor had advised. But the new baby decided to hang in, after all – at least it proved I had a tough-little-foetus, ready to brave adversity. I knew I should be grateful; I had a devoted husband, an adorable son and another baby on the way. And although I loved them all, I had begun to feel that my existence was essentially meaningless.

Chapter 9

One day, glancing casually out of the window, I saw David's boss's car draw up outside M Bossart's house. It was odd, because I'd noticed our neighbour leave for the office only a short while before. Mr Wilkinson, who was stout and had a big moustache, got out of the car. Though British by origin, he had spent his whole working life in the Congo and was a kind of honorary Belgian. In fact, he'd spent so long away from his native land that his English consisted of a string of outdated clichés. His French, which was fluent, was spoken with a Cockney accent. He rang the doorbell, and Mme Bossart duly appeared on the veranda in her satin dressing gown and feathered mules. There was a brief exchange before she took him indoors. Some time later, he came out of the house looking distinctly perky and pleased with himself, climbed into his car, and drove away.

It became a regular thing. Five minutes after the humble little sous-accountant had left for the office – I had taken to timing it – his boss, small and round and selfimportant, would arrive in the splendour that came with his position. There were no net curtains to twitch but, like a good suburban housewife, I kept a careful watch through my window. Naturally, I had no proof of what possibly went on underneath Madame's mosquito net. And whatever it was, it never went on for more than a quarter of an hour or so. But there was undoubtedly something taking place.

"Mr Wilkinson's having an affair with Mme Bossart," I told David one evening.

"Nonsense. You must be imagining it," he teased, as if such a thing were unthinkable.

And maybe, I told myself, I was. Perhaps Mr Wilkinson, whose wife had stayed at home in England, or Belgium, or wherever passed for home, just needed a cup of tea and a bit of sympathy. Certainly nothing dramatic happened, no shouting or scenes. M Bossart never came home unexpectedly, as he may have done in a novel. Far from being the torrid tropical romance I was hoping for, it was sublimely humdrum. We might have been living in Surbiton or Esher.

On Christmas Day we managed a brief escape. I had recently made friends with a woman called Erica, whom I'd met through Diana. Apart from having a daughter the same age as Charles, she was a South African, and she shared my abhorrence of apartheid. Having left her homeland, she had met and married Gerald, whose family owned a business in the Congo and who had been brought up here. They had invited us to lunch. Erica came to fetch us because Gerald – and this was long before men had started to occupy the kitchen – was doing the cooking. Even more impressively, they had let their servants off for the day.

Their house was magnificent. Sprawled on the hillside, it appeared to have grown organically rather than being built to a plan. As the family had expanded, they seemed to have added more buildings. The result was that each part of the house was at a different level, with its own particular vista. From the windows there were views not only of the river and the rocks and the wild African bush, but also of a beautiful garden. There were reminders of past grandeur, courtyards with Grecian urns spilling tropical flowers, as well as lawns and gardens with pools and fountains, and genuine Renaissance statues flaunting their naked bodies beside the bearded moss. Yet the house was being added to in an ongoing present. Gerald was proud of his particular contributions.

"I found this Congolese artist," he joked as he showed us around, pointing out the doors and pillars carved with African motifs, "and I kept him prisoner until he'd decorated every single piece of wood in sight." Although his family was Belgian, Gerald had been sent to school in England and sounded like an upper-class Englishman.

I pictured a black Bohemian, both slave and new-found friend. The sort of chap to whom Gerald would offer a gin and tonic after work in the evening. Though, come to think of it, if he'd kept him prisoner he'd also have had to give him dinner. I couldn't help wondering whether he'd slept in the European quarters or the "native" quarters. Gerald would have worked something out. He had the confidence of an old, established moneyed family.

For Christmas dinner, Gerald had concocted a dish of curried chicken and rice and a salad of pineapple and coconut and papaya, along with peanuts. It was deliberately ethnic and untraditional. We ate outside on the lawn in the open, and after lunch the children played beside the swimming pool, laughing as they sprayed one another with a hosepipe. The grown-ups joined in, chasing one another round the pool, and diving in and splashing each other. Drops of water glittered in the sunshine and, for the first time in ages, I felt released and happy.

Later, we walked down to the river. The immense Congo River, which hurled itself at this point over the rocks, creating a long chiffon scarf of white spume. Its growl, like the sea, was ever present. As we climbed down the hill and got closer, the sheer weight and power of that mightiest of mighty rivers had all the savagery and drama that I'd been longing to find ever since I'd got to the Congo. The vegetation below the house had deliberately been left wild, but there were paths that wended their way artfully down through the rocky terrain. Near the bottom, we came to a place where the undergrowth had been cleared. It was the original path used by the explorer Stanley. His expedition had had to hack their way through virgin jungle in order to carry their boats down-river, past the rapids. To be able to do this, they had built a road paved with rocks.

Gerald himself had discovered this piece of history, and I found it thrilling. I pictured the sweat and the toil and the fevers of the men as they dragged their equipment over those stones. They wouldn't have had a clue where they were heading or what they were going to find at the other end. Or, indeed, when the river, which they'd followed for a thousand miles, would become navigable again. What I didn't dwell on was the fact that those boulders would have been hauled by slaves. We were the heirs of a system which had used that labour without even thinking about it.

Our visit to Erica and Gerald whetted my appetite, once again, for the real Congo and its interior.

"If only," I said to David when we got back to our dreary little house in Léopoldville, "we could go upcountry." When he'd first been told about the job, David had been assured that we would spend only a few months in the capital while he reorganised the accounting system.

"Shouldn't be too long, now," David parried. The Company had mooted the idea of a post on a plantation called Lisala which was up-river, but this hadn't yet materialised. "It's up to Wilkinson."

"Wilkinson?"

"He is in charge of the department."

I despised Mr Wilkinson and David knew it.

"Once we get there," David assured me, "I'll be my own boss. I'll be responsible for the finances of an area of land the size of a European state."

I didn't really believe him. I was beginning to doubt everything I thought I knew. Part of me had started to wonder if perhaps I was making things up – like the improbable affair between Mr Wilkinson and Mme Bossart. "Upcountry" had become a sort of myth to me. I'd not only ceased to trust my feelings and instincts, I felt as if I was becoming increasingly cut off from the outside world. My little red Roberts wireless, which had been such a lifesaver in London, getting me through the tedium of the long cold winter when I'd been stuck in the flat with the baby, had proved useless here in the Congo. It was limited to long wave, and as the BBC World Service could only be picked up on short wave, I was reliant on hearsay to find out what was going on in the rest of the world. And although David would sometimes relay a piece of news when he got back from the office, the outside world, too, had begun to seem unreal.

I was also finding it more and more awkward communicating with Francois. I suspected him of lifting things, but, remembering the ugly scenes when food or objects went missing in Rhodesia, I dismissed my suspicions as paranoia. I had never been tidy, and having mislaid things, I would often come across them in unexpected places.

"Where's Charles's christening mug?" I asked David one day.

"Did we bring it?"

"I'm not sure." That was the trouble. I was not sure of anything any more.

Then, one morning while I was helping Francois make the bed, I thought I heard him say, "Je veux te baiser," while straightening the bottom sheet. He kept his head down so that all I could see were the grey curls on the top of his head and his sinuous arms and torso. I panicked. Could he really have said what I thought he had? Why was I letting him make my bed anyway? I knew enough colloquial French to know perfectly well that baiser didn't just mean a kiss.

I should perhaps have confronted Francois later, or told David. But as I couldn't be absolutely sure I'd heard right, I did neither. I just pretended that the whole thing hadn't happened. Apart from the fact that I reckoned David wouldn't believe me, I couldn't help thinking that it was partly my fault. By attempting to treat Francois as an equal I had probably been giving out the wrong messages.

It wasn't just that I was unsure of who I was and what I believed in, I was becoming increasingly negative. When the play-reading society had asked me to play Hermia in *A Midsummer Night's Dream*, I'd turned it down, using pregnancy as an excuse. In the old days I would have jumped at the opportunity to act. But, even though my bump was barely visible and I could in any case have worn loose clothes, I told myself and other people that there was no point because we might be going upcountry.

One Saturday at the club I spotted a young Englishwoman I'd never met before. An English rose with pale skin and marmalade-coloured hair. She was sitting outside on the veranda with her husband, and she was weeping into her lunch.

"I couldn't," she sobbed, pushing away a perfectly good steak au poivre. "I couldn't eat a thing."

Part of me was outraged at the waste of a good steak, while the other longed to make friends. It wasn't only that we came from the same sort of background. She was the wife of another young accountant who was working on one of the plantations up-river. He was a management trainee like David. We were bound to have a lot in common.

As it happened, I saw Caroline – for that was her name – the next day at a pre-lunch drinks party given by one of the Company wives. She appeared to know the hostess quite well. Rita was a typical hard-bitten expat. Someone I'd gone out of my way to avoid. In fact, I couldn't imagine why she'd asked us. Her husband had worked abroad for years and was due to retire soon. She had black hair with a grey streak along her parting, and nicotine-stained teeth.

"It's called a Black Lady," she joked as she handed out glasses of Guinness mixed with champagne – they were celebrating the arrival of their hamper – "but don't let that put you off." She had a deep throaty voice. "Besides, some men, I'm told, prefer their women that colour . . . like their coffee."

There were cries of "shame" and some titters. The joke was a colonial cliché.

Dismayed, I turned to talk to Caroline. I assumed that she too would have found the joke unpalatable, but she appeared to be indifferent. She was looking around her, almost vacantly.

I introduced myself and told her that I was also married to an accountant.

"Really?" I wasn't sure she'd taken in what I'd said. If she had, she wasn't interested. I tried various topics, including the Company furniture.

"Oh, yes," she said vaguely, "the curtains were so ghastly I got Peter Jones to make some new ones."

"How did you get them here?"

"I had them sent out by airmail."

I didn't remark that having them sent out by a London department store must have cost a fortune. Instead, I wished I could look like her and be like her and make those sorts of demands on my husband. She was so elegant, so beautiful, so English. But, try as I did, I couldn't manage to get through to her.

"We got married in Knightsbridge . . ." I overheard her sobbing later as she confided in our hostess. "My hairdresser came to the house . . ." Although Rita and Caroline came from totally different backgrounds, they appeared to have formed a real bond. "I never thought it would be like this . . ."

Rita clucked sympathetically.

"I just don't think I can take any more . . ."

"It's bloody hard, I know." Rita put her arms round Caroline. "But we've all been there, love, I promise you. We've just got to put up with things." It was exactly what my mother would have said. She had brought me up to endure. It wasn't just the "white man's burden", it was the woman's burden we colonial wives had to bear.

For all her racism, I realised that Rita was capable of real sympathy, and part of me wished that, like Caroline, I could have confided in her. But I knew my pride would never have allowed that. It was one thing turning on the waterworks in front of the immigration man in Johannesburg, but quite another showing the world what I was feeling. It would not only have exposed my vulnerability and failure, it would have meant acknowledging defeat. What I couldn't admit, even to myself, was that I envied Caroline because she was able to express what I felt like inside. Most of the women in Léopoldville, particularly the young ones, were probably in the same boat. We all wanted to open our mouths and howl. What none of us recognised, though, was the same need in others.

Chapter 10

I woke with a high temperature and a fiendish headache. This time I was properly ill. In a way, it came as a relief. It was something concrete. It let me off the hook and provided a focal point for my malaise. I decided that it must be flu and stayed in bed. At least in the Congo, I told myself, I could stay in bed. In England I would have had to cope somehow. The flu didn't get better. In fact, it got much worse. By day three I was floating in another world, a world devoid of all worries and responsibilities. On the fourth day, I suggested that David call the doctor. Without even bothering to do a test, the doctor diagnosed malaria.

"But I've been taking my pills," I said, even though I wasn't really certain.

He said nothing and injected a large syringe full of what I presumed was quinine into my bottom, or was it my arm? I was by this time so hazy I was barely taking things in. After that I slept . . . and slept . . . and slept. It was Saturday, and David and Charles went out to a lunch party; when they came back later in the afternoon, I didn't even hear them. I was dead to everything that was going on outside. But the stuff in the syringe had done its work. By that evening my temperature was down.

In a way, the malaria was a kind of salvation. It allowed me to retrieve myself. To prove that I had guts. I was not going to be defeated by a mere illness. I cast myself as the brave pioneering woman, a Mary Kingsley who cast aside such things. I got out of bed as soon as I could, determined to get on with life without any more fuss. The doctor had told me he'd have to see me again, so after a few days, I decided that rather than call him out I would go to the clinic.

It wasn't a very long walk, but it was a struggle. I was weaker than I'd realised. By the time I got there, I was exhausted. The doctor examined me and suggested a course of vitamin injections.

"Votre coeur est un peu faible," he threw out casually. Now I was not only the brave-little-woman and the pregnant-mum, but the wife-with-the-weak-heart as well. It was a romantic role, only too familiar in Victorian literature.

While we were having our lunch, I told David about my visit to the doctor. "He says I have a weak heart."

Suddenly I couldn't eat any more. I was hit by the fact that even I was mortal. Just saying the words had made my situation real. This was a part I didn't want to play. In novels, wives in the tropics frequently languished and then died. They left behind their children; their only memorial was a pathetic little headstone – a part of Africa that would remain forever England.

I'd never had panics before. My heart was fluttering so fast it was like the wings of a bird trapped in a greenhouse. I was that bird, and there was no way out of the glass prison into which I'd flown. I felt as if the world, my solid world, was about to come to an end. My body was so weak it seemed to be made of nothing but water.

"You'd better call a doctor," I gasped.

Once again, the doctor came immediately – one had to hand it to David, he'd been right about the Company looking after our physical welfare. The doctor felt my pulse and tested my blood pressure. It was so low that he had to give me digitalis. I knew all about the poison extracted from foxgloves. It was for hearts in distress. I had to be in extremis.

84

I have no idea whether I walked or was carried to the bedroom. What I do remember, though, was lying in my bed and looking through the netting of the window and knowing that I was dying. I no longer had the panics, but I felt unable to muster a thread of strength. Outside, the dappled shadows in the green trees looked unbearably beautiful. The mangoes were beginning to ripen and I would never eat them. I would never see Charles grow up. My life would be cut off before I'd had a chance to live properly. The world, even the Congo, seemed rich beyond measure. I felt an unendurable sorrow for myself, the young wife, about to leave it.

I didn't die. Of course I didn't. But once the panics, like the weevils in the rice, had laid their eggs in my being, they stayed. They had invaded the very cells of my body. Every evening as the sun plunged the world into darkness, I became reinfected. First the claustrophobia, then the panics, or was it the other way round? The two were intertwined. I would have to go outside. I didn't stand in the little garden with its balding lawn and the block of flats towering over it. I stood out in the open on the edge of the street, fighting for breath. All around me, the palm trees seemed to march in on me, suffocating me. I had no idea how I was going to survive.

I have subsequently discovered that panics are a well-known side effect of Paludrine, the drug we were swallowing every day. I had been given such a hefty dose when I was diagnosed with malaria that it was hardly surprising I manifested the symptoms. At the time, however, I didn't know this. As far as I was concerned, I had gone mad. "What on earth is a nervous breakdown?" my mother once asked, implying that it was no more than a self-inflicted state of mind. I was in an acute state of hypochondria. I'd become obsessed. My whole life had contracted. I couldn't think or concentrate on anything except my state of being.

85

My world was an unremitting blackness. All my presumptions about my sanity had been overturned.

Francois, sensing this state of affairs, asked if he could borrow some money. His small baby had died, he said, and he needed it for the funeral. Tears welled into his eyes. "Le pauvre petit cadavre," he said. I pictured the baby corpse, but this didn't move me. I didn't believe him. It wasn't just his phoney expression; some of the servants in Rhodesia had frequently used death as a means of extracting, or trying to extract, money from my parents. I told him that I would ask David.

"If the baby really has died," David argued, opening up a miasma of doubt, "and God knows, it wouldn't be surprising . . ."

So David gave Francois the money, and Francois was obsequious in his thanks. The funeral rites, he told us, would take a week.

One tiny incident at this time stays with me. For some reason, we had gone to a party given by some Americans. Our host put his arm around me.

"I just love pregnant women," he said kindly. It felt like a statement of pure, disinterested affection. To him, I was a person.

"What are you afraid of?" the doctor asked me when I went to see him for an antenatal check – the baby, despite tennis, malaria and panics, had miraculously stayed inside and continued to grow.

"Dying," I said.

He shrugged. "We are all afraid of dying." The doctor, a worldly man called Kokou, wasn't cold, just realistic. "You are not suffering from a psychosis," he went on. "In that case we would send you back to Europe. You are suffering from an anxiety state."

Anxiety state. I held onto that and tried to persuade myself that I wasn't mad or hysterical after all. I felt that I ought somehow to be able to use the surge of energy that came with the panics. In the olden days, I told myself, I'd have been called a witch. And in a primitive society I could have gone into a trance. I would have been able to dance, to transform myself. But in the civilised world of the nineteenth century, my state had been given the name of hysteria. It was unladylike, threatening to men. By the twentieth century I'd have been subjected to electrotherapy, or drugs, or both. Anything to tame me. I knew I was fortunate to be in the Congo and have Dr Kokou treating me.

None of that rationale, however, alleviated the symptoms. Every time the sun set and darkness descended, the world closed in on me. The panics would get so bad, my lungs felt as if they'd become paralysed. I no longer breathed automatically. I had to fight for every breath. In the bedroom at night, the ripe mangoes thudded down on the tin roof of our bungalow. We no longer went out in the evenings. To make matters worse, my friend, my substitute mother, Mrs Van Royan, had gone back to Europe. Her daughter's correspondence course had not been too successful. It wasn't just that Clara's education was suffering, Mrs Van Royan said, she needed other children to relate to.

We still saw Mr Van Royan, however. Strangely, my claustrophobia had not yet begun to trouble me in lifts, and because the Van Royans' elegant flat was high up, it was the one place I could relax. I found that the height and the view of the open, star-strewn sky outside on their balcony relieved my symptoms. I tried to explain my irrational fears to Mr Van Royan, but he was dismissive.

"If you had been in the war," he said, "you would know what it is to experience real fear." And of course I knew that, logically, he was right.

Interestingly, Thoby was more sympathetic. "If I were you I'd get out," he said. "This is a ghastly place, and there's no need for you to hang around. You could always go and stay with your parents in Iran."

But I couldn't do that. Apart from the fact that my mother also brushed off my panics – "Why don't you do your relaxation exercises?" she wrote – I couldn't just give up. I refused to be like those expat wives who used the excuse of their children's education or elderly parents to abandon their husbands.

David, meanwhile, was being kind. He had always been kind. And now that I was the little girl who needed protecting, he was extra kind. In fact, I suspected that he derived a certain satisfaction from my state. The neurotic-little-woman put him in a position of power. He had a role to play. He didn't mind my making excuses about going out. He'd never been a great one for socialising anyway – whenever I'd wanted to go out and have fun, he'd rather have stayed quietly at home. Besides, there wasn't much going on in Léopoldville at that time of the year. Many of the expats had gone back to Europe for Christmas and stayed on a while.

There was, however, one person who'd reversed the journey. Mr Wilkinson's wife had decided to spend the Christmas holidays with him and her son in the Congo – the chief accountant appeared to have a dynastic position, with a son in personnel. I'd expected someone hard-bitten and materialistic, a typical expat. But Mrs Wilkinson turned out to be square and sensible and motherly, with two fat plaits wound over the top of her head. She had a kind, moon-shaped face and she wore a gold cross round her neck.

There was another new arrival: a young Company wife. Her name was Pitou Mezzi, and she was Hungarian. She had a little boy called Zolica, who was exactly the same age as Charles. Her husband, Zoltan, was another of the Company's management trainees. Pitou and Zoltan had been at university during the 1956 anti-Communist uprising in their home country. She had been a drama student and he'd studied economics. Both had been on the streets and watched as tanks mowed down a bread queue. They had escaped together, leaving their respective families behind. After learning English, Zoltan finished his degree at an English university while Pitou did casual work to support him.

"We can't go back," Pitou told me matter-of-factly. As far as she was concerned, she was lucky to be alive and out of Hungary. The Congo was luxury in comparison to living under a Communist dictatorship.

I couldn't help liking and admiring Pitou, but I didn't particularly want to confide in her. She wouldn't have understood my malaise. It wasn't so much a thick skin she'd grown as an inner toughness. She had survived. In the end, that was what life was about, I'd concluded: survival.

Now, with Mrs Van Royan gone, the bridge games had ended – and with it our supply of eggs. I was incensed. Charles's nutrition continued to worry me, and I'd counted on them.

"It's not fair," I complained to David. "Sannie promised."

"Perhaps she doesn't come into town."

"She could always send them to the office with her husband."

"Why don't you use Flar?"

Flar was Mrs Van Royan's little dog who had always gone everywhere with her. She'd been worried that Flar would be lonely in the flat all day without a companion, so she'd left her with us.

"How?"

"Tell her that if you don't get the eggs you can't keep the dog."

It was so unlike David to suggest something like that that I gasped. It was also brilliant. I knew that Sannie didn't like dog hairs on her immaculate carpets. It took one phone call. She said her hens had stopped laying. I told her I didn't have enough food for the dog. We were both lying. Mrs Van Royan had left me with a stack of tins. And Sannie had eggs. I'd barely made a threat, and my supply was restored.

In the meantime, even though the darkness continued to descend every evening, I clung on. I felt as if I were like one of the vines in the jungle trying to clamber up to the light. I was helped by a radio lent to me by a friend who'd gone home to England on leave. The new radio was a more sophisticated one than mine. It had short wave. I spent hours turning knobs, searching the crackling airwaves for an English voice. Sometimes, very occasionally, I picked up the golden strains of the BBC's signature tune, the *Lillibullero*. Sometimes I even managed to hear bits of a play, or a talk. It proved that there was another world out there, that I wasn't alone.

One day while walking to the clinic, I bumped into Mr Van Royan. We hadn't seen him for weeks and he looked awful. It wasn't just his grey face – the whole of his body looked as if it had sunk inwards.

"What's the matter?" I exclaimed.

"I have high blood pressure," he explained. "It is an old trouble."

It was more than high blood pressure. I knew that. Without his wife, he was lost. I realised that his apparent lack of sympathy with my condition was because he'd had his own spectres to contend with. I was increasingly aware that practically everyone here in Léopoldville was living in their own private hell.

Chapter 11

David came home from the office one day and told me that we had been invited to dine with a visiting coffee planter who worked high up on the border with Rwanda-Burundi. He was on his way home on leave. They'd met at the club and the planter had suggested that we all eat at a restaurant out of town. David had managed to get hold of the Company car for the evening.

"You go."

"Won't you come too?"

"I can't."

"I thought you'd like him."

"I know, but . . ."

"He's your kind of person, and it's a nice place."

It was the idea of getting out of the city that swung it. The restaurant stood in a large, open area. There were no all-encroaching palm trees and the dining room was large and airy.

I liked the planter. He talked about the life he lived, the space and the solitude. "I don't think I could contemplate anything else now," he said.

I pictured the slopes covered by coffee plants, a backdrop of mountains, and a vista stretching out over the undulating landscape. The man gave off a sense of calm that I found comforting. He belonged to a world that I understood: a world of decent standards, of order, where everything fell into place.

And then, while we were waiting for our orders to arrive, it happened.

I'm not sure whether it was the setting of the sun, or the vision of that coffee plantation high up in the rolling hills, but I began to feel the familiar flutter. The world started to close in on me and I began to be afraid that I would not be able to breathe. I hung on as long as I could. I began to lose the feeling in my hands, then my arms started to feel paralysed.

"I've got to go to the lavatory," I lied. "You get on without me." I had no idea what I was going to do; all I knew was that I had to get out, otherwise I would surely die.

I stood outside the restaurant, just as I always stood outside our house, and tried to pull myself together. Perhaps it was because I had delayed escaping out into the open, battling with myself, not wanting to appear silly, not wanting to let David down, that in this instance going back into that restaurant seemed well-nigh impossible. I tried to think of the most frightening thing I'd ever had to do. Once, when I was about seven years old, one of the grown-ups had bet me that I wouldn't have the courage to jump off the top board into the swimming pool. I remembered standing on that board with the water impossibly far below, and agonising. Then I'd flung away all instinct for self-preservation, held my nose, and jumped.

I stood on the edge of the abyss that night with the sky arcing above me and knew that I had to do the same thing. Even if it cost me my life, I would have to go back into that restaurant. I tried to take a deep breath, battled to still my beating heart, and went in. And although I could barely touch the food – a little fish with mashed potatoes and peas – and I was too distracted to join in the conversation, I survived. The panics certainly didn't stop after that, but the fact that I had of my own volition defied my fear, helped. However bad things felt, I knew after that that I could ultimately take control.

When we got home that evening David and I talked about the planter and his coffee plantation. It had all sounded so idyllic, being high up in the mountains, that we had both been temporarily transported out of the torpid heat of Léopoldville.

"I don't know why," I remarked, "but I've always loved the idea of tea plantations."

"It's all that land," David replied. "It must be a basic instinct. Looking out over your own land."

"You're probably right." I hadn't spoken about "upcountry", but that must have been in both our minds because David suddenly broke.

"We've got to get out."

"What do you mean?"

"I'm doing the sort of work I did when I first started my articles."

It was the first time David had allowed himself to let go, and once it started, it all came out. Mr Wilkinson, he told me, wasn't even a qualified chartered accountant. His systems were as antiquated as his English. What's more, he'd claimed to have no knowledge of David's brief to reorganise the system. As far as he was concerned, his accounts worked the way they were and he certainly wasn't going to change anything.

I wasn't really surprised. The organisation in the Company was probably as chaotic as in the country as a whole. I'd already come to the conclusion that the much-vaunted management trainees were in fact little more than a source of cheap labour. Anyone, I suspected, could have done either Thoby or David's job. But not everyone would have been willing to put up with conditions in the Congo. The Company had exploited people's appetite for adventure.

"Everything will be all right when we get upcountry," I comforted David.

"If we ever get there." It was the first time he had admitted any doubts.

"Of course we will." I didn't believe it myself, but I had to persuade David. I realised that it was something we'd both been clinging to all along. Once we were upcountry, I would find my real Congo and he would be in charge of his own district and everything would be all right.

"I'll insist. I'll tell Wilkinson that unless I get offered a post upcountry, I'll consider resigning."

David's new-found determination paid off. Within weeks he was told that he would definitely be going up to Lisala, the plantation up in the Haut-Congo.

It was George, the driver, who told me about the troubles. George was always the first to know everything. It was he who had announced President Kennedy's assassination. "Mort," he'd declared. "Assassiné." And for a moment or two I hadn't believed him. How could he possibly know about the American president? Now he was telling me about the Simbas.

"There is trouble there because of Lumumba. That is where he comes from. His people believe that he was killed by the Americans. That is why they want to kill all the white people."

"You don't believe that, do you?"

George shrugged. "Why was he killed? Who killed him? We have questions, but no answers."

He was right there. Although there'd been rumours about Lumumba being killed when he tried to escape from Katanga, his body had never been found. But the idea of the Americans actually murdering Lumumba was scarcely credible. It seemed much more likely that the prime minister had been bumped off by the disaffected people of Katanga. I also felt sure that George was exaggerating about the Simbas wanting to kill all the white people. That sounded far too melodramatic.

David confirmed George's information when he came home that evening.

"There's been an uprising against the government led by a man called Pierre Mulele in the Kivu and Eastern Province," he said. "The United Nations are sending in troops to deal with it."

"George seems to think that the Americans killed Lumumba," I told David.

"You can hardly blame the CIA for wanting to get rid of him."

"What do you mean?"

"Lumumba was importing Russian ammunition."

"Oh, I know that . . . but surely if Lumumba wasn't getting the UN help he needed –"

"It's well known that the USSR is dying to get a foothold in Africa."

"Sounds to me like 'Reds under the beds'."

"It's power politics, if that's what you mean. That's what the Cold War is all about."

It was hard to argue against David's implacable logic.

"I wouldn't be surprised if it was Russia that's behind the troubles in the Haut-Congo," he went on.

"Isn't the plantation we're supposed to be going to in the Haut-Congo?"

"Well . . . yes." There was a pause. "That's what I was going to tell you."

Lisala, it seemed, was right in the heart of the uprising. The Company had had to evacuate all the personnel. It meant that we wouldn't be going upcountry after all.

Thoby, as ever, knew all about what was going on. "Simba means lion," he told us with glee. "They paint their faces white. That way, they think they'll be like us."

"But they don't like us."

"That may be true, but we've got what they want. It's all very primitive, you see. They believe in witch doctors and black magic." Thoby laughed, but I noticed that David didn't join in.

"We've got to get out of Léopoldville," I said to David after Thoby had gone home. It felt as if our whole future were at stake. I knew that I couldn't hold on if we stayed in Léopoldville. "It doesn't matter about Lisala. You could go to another plantation."

"If the rebellion spreads –"

"It won't spread." I truly believed that most people were well meaning and that democracy would win in the end. "And anyway, what about the UN? They have to have a reason to be here . . ."

I knew that David was, if anything, even more disappointed than I was about not going to Lisala. It wasn't just that he'd have a more responsible job; for him, part of this African adventure was getting into the bush.

"I'll see what I can do." He clenched his jaw as if preparing for battle. He hated confrontations, but having a neurotic wife was undoubtedly making David more masterful.

"Have you seen my gold cuff links?" he asked as we were getting ready to go to bed.

"No. Why?"

"I haven't seen them since the Queen's Birthday Party. I assumed you'd put them away somewhere, as they're not in any of my drawers." Unlike me, David was an immaculately tidy person. He always kept things in their proper place.

"Perhaps Francois has taken them."

"He wouldn't have done that."

"I don't trust him."

"Nonsense."

The next day David asked Francois about the cuff links. Francois said he'd look for them. They didn't turn up that day, but the next day, when David had gone to the office, Francois took me into the bedroom and pointed them out to me. The box was at the back of the drawer where David normally kept them.

"They weren't there before," David said.

"Maybe you just didn't see them. Or you moved them?"

"Of course I didn't. You must have –"

"It's Francois," I screamed, "can't you see? Can't you see what's happening under your nose? He's been taking you for a ride. It's because you're English. You're white. Don't you understand?"

There was a ghastly silence.

"He'll have to go," David said quietly.

"Francois?" I was frantically scrabbling to do an about-turn; to unsay what I'd just said. "I didn't mean –"

". . . we can't have someone we can't trust."

"But the six children –"

"I know."

In a way it was a relief, on two counts. David had taken the decision and I felt vindicated. In another way it was awful, as we had the fate of another human being in our hands. Despite Provis's claims that the whole of Léopoldville were falling over themselves to employ Francois, we knew he wouldn't get another job.

"Can't we give him a warning?" It was me this time who was pleading.

"I suppose so. I'll give him a couple of months' notice. We should be gone after that."

I heard David talking to Francois. He may have acquired the superficial trappings of the colonial male, but he was still essentially English. He wasn't, at heart, callous. He sounded too polite. Too English. Almost apologetic. I knew that we'd made a mistake in not keeping to our resolve, especially as Francois treated me with cold disdain from then onwards, but the alternative was too awful to contemplate.

Soon after that, we were visited by one of Francois's ex-employers who happened to be in the Congo temporarily. The man, a Belgian, greeted Francois like a brother, flinging his arms round his ex-employee. They chatted away in French. It was a completely different master–servant relationship. Their bonhomie rubbed salt into my already wounded psyche. We had not only failed ourselves, we had failed Francois.

I thought about George's remarks about the Americans killing Lumumba. It didn't seem likely. On the other hand, the Soviets had started courting Lumumba . . . And what about the Belgians? Where did they stand? They appeared to be very reluctant to let go. America was sending aid and buying influence. The Russians, I'd been told, were waiting in Brazzaville, ready to pounce. Even the Chinese, it was rumoured, were trying to get a toehold. What chance did the Congolese people have while the powerful nations of the world were carving up Africa in the same way European colonial powers had done in the nineteenth century? The Congolese were being bribed and bulldozed by whoever had the most money. My dreams about the autonomy of the people of the newly independent Congo were beginning to look very naïve.

It wasn't long before David was offered another job. This time it was a plantation called Alberta. I looked it up on the map. The place was surrounded by little grass symbols that I knew from my school geography meant marshland.

"We can't go there," I told David.

"Why not?"

"It wouldn't be safe for Charles."

"But I can't turn it down."

"Well, I'm not going." I'd forgotten all my fine resolutions of sticking by my husband's side even if it meant wading through mangrove swamps or hacking our way through the jungle with my baby on my back.

David did turn Alberta down, but insisted that he wanted to be sent to another plantation. I had no idea whether he blamed his refusal on his neurotic wife. I no longer cared.

Soon afterwards, David managed to borrow a car from the Company. It was ours for the whole weekend. We chose to drive to a beauty spot several miles out of Léopoldville. It was where the Belgians had taken their families in "the good old days before Independence". The place, which had a dam and picnic areas, was otherwise unremarkable. But at least it was out of town and we had it to ourselves, and that alone was a treat.

On the way home, we decided to go off the main road to explore a bit more of the countryside. David had managed to get hold of a detailed map and looking at it, the road appeared to go through a village before linking up with another minor road and rejoining the highway. Very soon, the so-called road deteriorated to a dirt track, but we drove on. Having got the car, we were determined to make full use of it. David was a good driver and had an exceptional sense of locality. He also had faith in maps. They made his world ordered and predictable, and therefore safe. If the map told him something was somewhere, he knew it was. And because his world was safe, mine was too. But as we drove deeper into the forest I began to get apprehensive.

"Let's go back," I said. Charles was getting restless and hungry.

"Can't be far now," David said, "and then we'll meet up with the other road." Once he got it into his head to do something, he needed to see it through. I fed Charles a banana and cuddled him as he fell asleep.

Dusk fell and we were catapulted from the gloaming into complete darkness. With the darkness came my panics. "Please," I said, "couldn't we just stop so that I can get out of the car for a moment?"

"That wouldn't be safe," he said. "You never know what sort of snakes or animals are out there." He had put his lights on to full beam and they picked out the ruts in the road and the looming, seemingly impenetrable jungle.

David drove on. I was battling not only with my own panics, but I sensed also that he was beginning to get seriously worried. I could feel it. It was contagious. And his fear, which seemed to supersede mine, was a fear of the elemental, a fear of the unknown.

"Let's turn round."

"There's no room." He was right. The jungle came right up to the edge of the narrow road.

And then, in the distance, we heard the faint sound of drums and chanting. The sound of human beings. David drove on and then stopped. We had reached a village. It was in semidarkness. Apart from our headlights, the only other light came from small fires outside the huts and a larger fire in the middle of a bare space. In the shadows beyond the black shapes of the mud huts was the jungle. It loomed menacingly all around us. The shapes of figures, barely discernible in the darkness, appeared to be moving. I seemed to make out something that looked like a bier near the fire, with a bundle lying on top. It may not have been a dead body, but I was convinced it was. Standing round it was a group of people. The chanting and drumming appeared to be coming from them.

"I think they're having a wake," I whispered. I could smell death.

"We'd better get out." There was real panic in David's voice now. He switched on the engine, backed the car, and then slewed round and drove away along the same road at high speed, careless of the ruts and bumps. We didn't say anything to one another. I had never seen David shaken like that before. I also felt as if we'd violated something sacred.

We got home to find that the front door had been smashed. Inside,

100

there was chaos. Our house had been ransacked and our possessions strewn everywhere. The internal doors, which had been locked, were broken open, leaving splintered wood on the floor. Surprisingly, despite the vandalism, not that many things had been stolen. The thieves appeared to have been after gadgets and machines. To my great distress, my two most precious possessions, my typewriter and my Roberts radio, were missing. They had also taken the short-wave radio we'd borrowed.

We telephoned Thoby and he agreed that there wasn't much point in phoning the police.

"I'll tell the Company in the morning," David said. "At least we were insured."

"Do you think it was Francois?"

"What?"

"He was the only person who knew we were going out for the whole day. He could have tipped them off." I wasn't being entirely paranoid. Ever since he had propositioned me while making the bed, Francois had been surly and uncooperative. I knew he blamed me for the confrontation over the missing cuff links.

David didn't argue. We were both learning to deal with the fact that anything might happen.

Soon after the robbery the Company came up with another job on a plantation. This one was called Elizabetha. It was also in the Haut-Congo, but in a part where there was no trouble. The plantation was about one hundred and fifty miles down-river from the town of Stanleyville. As there were no little grass symbols on the map in that area, I said I'd go, and David accepted the job. After that, all we had to do was pack up our belongings, which would be taken up-river by paquebot – paddle steamer. We would follow in an aeroplane.

On our last evening, David and I were sitting on the veranda when we heard music floating over from the house opposite. Knowing that we were at last getting out, and freed of our possessions, which were on their way up-river, we were in a mellow mood. It was a song from the First World War, a scratchy seventy-eight being played on an old-fashioned wind-up gramophone. Under the dim, insect-ridden lights two couples were dancing. In my memory the picture is softened, its details blurred by the mosquito netting so that it looks almost romantic. Amorous Mr Wilkinson clasping his mistress proudly to his paunchy frame steps out boldly, while in the shadows skinny M Bossart holds his boss's virtuous wife at a suitably correct distance. They weave in and out of the light, circling round and round the tiny veranda.

Why do I remember the scene so vividly? The sound of the gramophone . . . the shadowy figures of two middle-aged couples circling round one another . . . the night sky . . . the smell of the tropics . . . and that song.

Old soldiers never die, never die, never die,
Old soldiers never die, they simply fade away.

Was it because I longed to join in, or because part of me mourned the passing of an era? Probably both. But more importantly, it was the illusion – an illusion that we were all unwittingly clinging to – that this life of privilege could go on forever. I thought of the fragility of life. Of course old soldiers die. They may linger on in people's memories, but still, death itself was horribly final. And on this continent, the end was invariably swift and often brutal.

PART II

Chapter 12

In the late nineteenth century, Joseph Conrad made his way up the Congo River by boat. In his time, Stanleyville had been the centre of evil, the pulse of the slave trade. "The horror," Conrad has Kurtz say in his *Heart of Darkness*. "The horror." I imagined that the blood and chains and amputated limbs would have left their mark on the earth, that one might catch the sound of those victims' screams in the foetid atmosphere. I had always prided myself on picking up atmospheres, yet in Stanleyville I didn't feel any of it. In fact, I liked the place. It was partly, of course, the sheer relief of getting away from Léopoldville. But it was something more, too. The modern world with all its plastic and prestressed concrete hadn't yet taken over here, and Stanleyville was relatively untouched. As for the atmosphere, it was as if time had sterilised the past. As smells and rot disappear from an old compost heap, so memories had faded. The present was what counted.

And there was something else, too. The jungle, the old houses built on stilts – whether to deter snakes, or because people believed that mosquitoes were unable to fly above a certain height – carried resonances of my past. In some indefinable way, I found it all comforting. And I can only put these feelings down to my ancestors. The Africans worship theirs. Mine had been colonisers and empire builders. It was deeply unfashionable to admit such a thing in the Sixties but, whether I liked it or not, it was a fact. And my forebears were part of me, encoded in my genes. The old colonial town had stirred some ancestral memory. Yet just as I had no bad feelings from the past, I had no intimations or sinister forebodings about the future either.

We were staying overnight in the Company rest house before flying off to the plantation the next day. That evening we dined in a restaurant jutting out over the Congo River. It is an evening that has stayed with me. I can still picture the platform we were sitting on, see the lights reflected and refracted on the moving water. Above all, I recall the vastness of the Congo River as it flowed across half a continent to the distant ocean. It promised, as rivers and railways do, possibilities. Another kind of life. A different tomorrow. But another reason the evening has stayed with me is because Stanleyville was to become so pivotal in later events.

The food was delicious and plentiful. Good Belgian cooking, fresh fish caught from the river, and French wine. We were all in high spirits. With us was Dr Kokou who, as chief medical officer, periodically visited the various Company plantations. He'd been to Stanleyville many times before and, as far as I could tell, he welcomed the escape from his clinic in Léopoldville, regarding these jaunts as something of a holiday. He had invited some friends to join us. They were a young Belgian couple; the wife, like me, was pregnant.

"Where are you going to have your baby?" she asked me.

"On the plantation. And you?"

"I'm not sure. They say I should go back to Belgium . . . for the first."

"Everything will be fine," I reassured her as if I were an old hand at the business. "Everything's so safe nowadays. There's nothing to worry about."

Later, I was to run and rerun that fragment of conversation. She was so young. Even younger than me.

It was the first time we had socialised with Belgians, and Dr Kokou's presence automatically ensured our acceptance. Although the conversation between me and the young wife was relatively trivial, the mere fact that we were both pregnant established something of a bond. We vowed to keep in touch. Elizabetha wasn't far away, I declared, no real distance in African terms. Our new babies would meet up, make friends. Like the river, the conversation ebbed and flowed and washed away into the darkness of that warm, mellow night, while a new life lay ahead of us.

The next morning we learned that the small plane we were supposed to be travelling in had something wrong with its engine. Normally it carried the weekly mail and landed in a place called Basoko, which was on the other side of the river from Elizabetha. The breakdown meant we would have to travel to the plantation by boat instead. The men were impatient about the delay. There was a great deal of talking and stamping of feet while they fixed up an alternative form of transport. But I was thrilled. I'd always loved journeys – letting go, surrendering myself to fate – and river journeys in particular. While the men re-arranged our trip and negotiated with the boatmen, Charles and I played in the mud at the edge of the river.

We set off at about ten o'clock in the morning in a baleinière, a small, high-sided whaling boat. It was used to transport the post as well as all the goods and equipment that were needed by the small mission stations and plantations down-river from Stanleyville. This meant that after all the paraphernalia had been loaded, we had to perch wherever we could on engine parts and tractor wheels. Not that it mattered. Charles, who would never have stayed still in any case, could clamber around fairly safely on the high-sided boat. He had with him his much-abused teddy bear, as well as a silk scarf of mine that he stroked for comfort.

Powered by a primitive engine, the boat set off chug-chugging in a leisurely fashion down the Congo River. Even at this point, a thousand miles up-river from Léopoldville, the Congo was so wide that it was impossible to see from one side to the other, and the driver had to navigate his way through a maze of islands. The sun was shining, a breeze was blowing, and I was happy. Occasionally we passed a fishing village, a small cluster of huts on the riverbank. These were a mere nibble out of the wilderness of jungle that stretched away and beyond the imagination.

There were no sounds besides the chug of the engine, no indication of the wildlife teeming inside the forest. From time to time we would see a man standing in a pirogue that had been hollowed out from the trunk of one of the trees. He manoeuvred it with such dexterity that his oar looked like a part of his body. If I'd thought about it, I would have realised that it must have been somewhere round here that Conrad's steamer had been attacked by little black men with their poisoned arrows. Nothing, though, was further from my mind. As we wove on down-river past sand-banks and palm trees and river jungle, layers of anxiety sloughed off me like dead skin. I felt more at peace than I had for years.

After travelling for several hours, the boat turned off to one side and chugged towards the riverbank. It pulled up beside a jetty and the driver turned off the engine. For a moment there was utter silence. Then, to my amazement, we were greeted by a red-headed man who came pounding down to the jetty to collect the goods being delivered to him. He had a Scottish accent and seemed just as surprised to see us as we were to see him.

"You must come up to the house for a cup of tea," he said after we had introduced ourselves. He exuded energy and vitality.

The driver was doubtful. Time was short, he told us, he was planning to drop the mail at a couple more stations and then come back the next day. But the Scotsman was insistent.

"My wife would be so disappointed if you didn't," he said to me. "She hasn't seen another European woman for months."

Grudgingly, our driver agreed to a short break.

The Scotsman turned out to be a medical missionary, and his wife was yet another English rose, wilting in the heat. Together with their baby daughter, they lived in a small, simple bungalow down near the river. While we were drinking our tea, we were joined by a newly qualified doctor from overseas.

The missionary had been right. His wife desperately needed another woman to talk to. Over tea and scones, she told me about her daughter who was in fact two and a half years old, and hadn't yet shown any inclination to walk. And indeed the girl, a fine, fat child with blonde curls, seemed perfectly happy sitting on a grass mat, smiling blandly at the world, while Charles, a year younger, was running around, climbing up and into everything.

"Is it normal?" she fretted. It seemed to me highly abnormal, but I didn't say so.

"Do you think I should take her home to see a specialist?"

"I don't know." I wasn't yet twenty-six. How could I possibly know?

"A specialist in London. He'd be bound to know." London seemed very far away.

Living in such absolute isolation with, it seemed, only the occasional boat calling in, it must have been impossible to put anything into proper perspective. Her husband and his young helper were out all day, ministering not only to the souls but also to the bodies of black babies far more urgently in need of help. It can't have been of much comfort to her.

"Have some more tea . . . another scone. You could stay the night . . ." she pleaded when the driver came up to the house to tell us we had to leave. It was like a tug of war. In many ways, I would have dearly liked to stay, but our driver was adamant. We still had a long way to go. It was difficult and dangerous navigating the vast waterway in darkness, and he wanted to reach our destination before nightfall.

We set off again down the river, and glancing back, I saw the three of them, two men and a woman with a baby in her arms, waving from the makeshift quay. Tiny specks of white in a wilderness of black.

I looked down at the water hyacinth: floating islands, mats of vegetation. This pretty, innocuous little mauve flower, originally from South America, had become, we'd been told, a real menace. It clogged up the river, raising the water level, and was impossible to get rid of. It struck me that human beings were much the same. They came to foreign countries and tried to establish themselves. While some died, others flourished. They multiplied and imposed their customs and values on the local people, changing the balance and way of life forever.

I had supposed that with Independence and the removal of most Belgians, the indigenous people of the Congo, who now had room to breathe and grow, would flourish. But it wasn't as simple as that. The old colonial powers had been replaced by new international powers that were battling to get their hands on the country's riches. And even though the missionaries we'd just visited were curing diseases and saving lives, their ultimate motive was also gain – Congolese souls. Yet there didn't seem much point in being censorious. From time immemorial, people had changed, and been changed by, the foreign countries they passed through or lived in. Empires had come and gone as a consequence. The water hyacinth, which was taking over the river and changing the environment, must surely eventually choke itself, or die off from disease.

"Comme il est beau," I exclaimed as the sun started to sink, staining the river orange.

Dr Kokou laughed, calling me "une anglaise romantique". The men had taken to making fun of me and my enthusiasm for "the beauties of nature". For them, the sun merely rose and set, and the river ran inevitably to its destination.

The driver revved the engine and Dr Kokou asked him how far it was to the plantation. I had become so much part of the flow of the river that I had forgotten we were meant to hurry. The driver pushed the fat little baleinière as fast as it could go, but still, the tension grew. Night was falling rapidly, and with only one light to navigate by, our helmsman had increasingly to rely on memory. I pictured us getting stuck on a sandbank and having to spend the night on the crocodile-infested river. At one stage, I heard what I imagined to be the death throes of some animal. Charles started to cry because he was getting hungry. Water and jungle loomed all around us in the rapidly growing gloom. Everyone kept silent as the little boat kept chugging through the unfamiliar water.

It was completely dark by the time we reached the plantation where we were to spend the night. Only the glimmer of a torch punctuated the blackness. The owner, who had seen the light of our boat, was already there to greet us. His torch picked up the dark spikes of reeds growing beside the bank and the black, slimy wood of the landing stage. With him were a couple of Africans who waded into the water and helped pull the boat in. Monsieur – I never did discover what his name was – seemed unperturbed by the fact that we were so late. He was warm and welcoming; a tall figure in the darkness, with a strong handshake. As it was too dark to attempt to unpack the boat, he arranged accommodation for the driver before leading us along a damp footpath through long grass till we reached an old colonial bungalow. It was sheltered by huge trees, part of the original forest. The light of a hurricane lamp glowed from its square windows.

Dr Kokou had already explained that our host was a vieux colon, and

111

that he owned and ran his own plantation. With most of the plantations now owned by corporations, these people were the last of a kind, he'd told us, and theirs was a way of life that was rapidly coming to an end. Madame, a woman in late middle age, was on the veranda waiting to greet us. There was an air of tranquillity about her that reminded me of the early American pioneers. Lit by the soft light from a hurricane lamp, she emanated serenity.

For her eight-year-old daughter, Brigitte, our arrival seemed almost unbearably stimulating. She had clearly been talking of nothing else all day. The child fell upon Charles and couldn't stop kissing him. Chattering away, she showed us where we would be sleeping. Would it be all right, she asked, if Charles moved into her bedroom? I warned her mother that he might keep her awake. But that didn't worry anyone and the cot was moved into Brigitte's room. She was so excited to have the company of another child that she bounced up and down on her bed, her thick blonde plaits flying up with each jump. It was the attraction of one young animal to another, and Charles, who was revelling in all the attention, jumped up and down in his cot, sharing in her enthusiasm. Long after they were supposed to have gone to bed we could hear Brigitte chattering away to him in French.

We dined at the kitchen table. It was a simple meal. The family were almost completely self-sufficient. Madame baked her own bread and grew her own vegetables, and there was fish to be had in abundance from the river. But what struck me most as I looked at their faces lit by the guttering candle, was how truly themselves they both were. Living in this rare isolation, unaffected by the rest of so-called civilisation, they had developed into unique individuals; they seemed to have established a system of living in harmony both with one another and their surroundings. Over a bottle of wine that Dr Kokou had brought, they told

112

us about their way of life. Predictably, it was the independence that they valued most of all. They were answerable to no one but themselves. They didn't care about the heat or the mosquitoes, or indeed any of the minor inconveniences. Their plantation was home, and they had no desire to go back to Europe.

Monsieur had been brought up on this very plantation, which his father had owned before him. Their older children, they said with a certain regret, had chosen to live in Belgium and make a life for themselves there. It was understandable. There was no real future here. It wasn't just Independence, everything was changing. There was a new world order and it was becoming increasingly difficult to operate alone. Everything now was owned by large companies like the one David was working for. Soon, they told us, Brigitte would have to go away to school and she, too, would not come back. It wasn't just the loss of their children and a way of life that saddened them. Unless he died in harness, they knew that when Monsieur was too old to work they would not be able to go on living here either. There was a Chekhovian feeling to it all, a nostalgia that comes with nightfall and inevitable endings.

Nevertheless, our hosts were anxious to find out what was happening in the rest of the world. We were outsiders and they wanted to know if we had heard anything, particularly about the current situation in the Haut-Congo. It was the sort of conversation that never took place in Léopoldville – at least, not when I was around. As neither Monsieur nor Madame spoke English, the talk had necessarily been in French, and although I couldn't understand a lot of what was being said, I managed to pick up the gist.

It was les jeunesse, I gathered, the young people, who were the source of the trouble. And, as I had already learned, their leader was Pierre Mulele, who was said to be fomenting the discontent among them. He'd already instigated the uprising in the Haut-Congo – the uprising that had prevented us from going to Lisala – and only le bon Dieu knew where he'd stop. Mulele was, I gathered, an ex-minister who'd served under Patrice Lumumba. He was discontented, Monsieur said, because he'd had power taken away from him. "C'est normal." It was only to be expected that with their new freedom, everyone wanted to be top dog. Mulele had been trained in Beijing and it was the Chinese who were giving him funds to "destabilise the region". Also, he deliberately played on the superstitions of the people.

"The young men take hallucinogenic substances," Monsieur was saying, "and that makes them think they are invulnerable."

Perhaps I should have been more worried. The troubles weren't that far away from Elizabetha, where we were going. But, sitting round their rough-hewn table in the semidark, it was difficult to feel alarmed. Both Monsieur and Madame had a strength of character and a stature about them that was peculiarly comforting. They lived by their own values. They had created a feeling of safety, the inviolability of hearth and home. Or at any rate, that was how I felt in the drowsy warmth of that slightly inebriated evening.

The next day, however, I realised that they were vulnerable like all of us. The plantation, it transpired, was on an island, one of the many islands in the Congo River. While Monsieur was taking us round his estate in his boat, I heard him confiding in Dr Kokou. He was sorry to trouble him, he said, but he had this chronic pain in his stomach and he wasn't sure whether it was serious or not. I could tell that it was hard for this proud man to ask for help. The doctor was sympathetic. He said it was impossible to tell without an examination. But in any case, he told Monsieur, with a chronic stomach pain it was essential to see a specialist. It made me realise the risk inherent in the life they were living. Apart from the possibility that Monsieur may have been suffering from cancer, there was the danger of a sudden haemorrhage from a stomach ulcer. There was also, of course, the possibility of a serious accident or their child becoming suddenly ill. They were a whole day's journey from Stanleyville.

We set off in our baleinière later that morning after breakfast. The warm mist rising from the jungle made it look ethereal. Once again we were in a timeless place, in the middle of a timeless continent, chugging slowly down a timeless river. Once again, apart from watching Charles, I had the leisure to think and dream. It struck me that the couple we had just stayed with, living all alone on that island in the Congo River, were, in their way, very like some of the old colonials in Rhodesia. They, too, lived on isolated farms in the middle of the bush. They, too, had to cope with adversity. And invariably, they did so with courage and without fuss. They, too, had clung fiercely to their independence, the freedom to be themselves, and, despite the hazards, they wouldn't have traded their way of life for any other.

As a teenager, I had labelled them all as bigots and racists. And many of them were. But what the vieux colons we had just been staying with had shown me was that any individual choosing to live this sort of life was courageous. The fact that the vieux colons were of a different nationality and spoke a different language meant that I had not automatically judged them. They may well have been politically incorrect, they were certainly an anachronism, uselessly fighting the tides of history, but they were worthwhile as people. I was being forced to face the contradictions of what was happening in the new Africa.

The next place we called at was a small plantation that belonged to a minor corporation. Once again, we were met by the manager of the plantation. He was a young man, a nouveau colon. His hair was cropped almost to the scalp, he wore short shorts, and his leg muscles were like the exposed roots of a tree. His extreme shyness made him talk compulsively with such a heavy, guttural accent I couldn't understand what he was saying. While the men unloaded the tractor wheels, he took us to his house, an ugly little brick bungalow close to the beach. It was a bleak place, within yards of the factory. Having introduced us to his wife, the planter took David and Dr Kokou off on a tour of his workplace, leaving me and Charles in the house.

The wife was very young, little more than a child, stick-skinny and in a state of extreme neurosis. She had a baby, a little girl, who was playing on the floor. Without even bothering to acknowledge me, the wife snatched the bundle of letters we had brought with us and fled to her bedroom, locking the door behind her. I was left alone in the bleak sitting room with two infants. The place, it seemed to me, was as close to hell as it is possible to imagine. The air was permeated by a smell reminiscent of dirty underclothes – I later discovered it was the palm fruit boiling – and the factory was so close that there was a perpetual din. It was a nonstop thud . . . thud . . . thud . . . as the nuts were pounded into pulp to extract the oil.

The baby, who was about a year old, seemed to have been affected by this nightmarish atmosphere, as she was a little savage. As soon as the door was closed, she took one look at Charles and, scuttling across the concrete floor on her hands and knees, bit him with her sharp little baby teeth. Having scooped up my yowling child, I sat on the unyielding seat of a chair covered with some sort of plastic material, waiting, as at the dentist's, for the noise of the drill to cease, and for something to happen.

At one o'clock on the dot, the pounding at the factory stopped. A few minutes later, the plantation manager and his visitors came back to the house. They brought with them a whiff of normality, a palpable sense of relief. Unlike his wife, the young planter was quite cheerful. He was no longer shy, and he offered us some beer and made an effort to dispel the air of desolation that pervaded the house. Eventually his wife reappeared; her face was blotchy, her eyes red with crying. We all sat down at a small, rickety table covered with a plastic cloth. She neither talked nor ate as she toyed with her leathery steak and soggy frites – the lettuce had already died in a sea of vinaigrette.

I found the situation both scary and rather too close to home. It was the state I'd been afraid of getting into in Léopoldville. Although I made an effort to talk to her, she had erected an impenetrable barrier. Alone in her jungle madness, it couldn't be long, surely, before she broke and started gibbering like an idiot and sticking pins into herself, or, like one isolated manager I'd heard of, eating the soap powder. It was such a desperate situation, such a living purgatory, that all I could feel was a wave of almost hysterical relief when we got away from that bungalow. I had never before been in such close contact with terminal despair. The machines had started up again as soon as the lunch hour was over, and, as I pictured their thud, thud, thud banging remorselessly on that poor woman's brain, I knew that I couldn't have endured it.

Although we'd been travelling for a day and a half, we were in fact only halfway to Elizabetha. Our baleinière, however, having delivered all its goods, was set to head back up to Stanleyville. We were to complete our journey not in the trusty, familiar old tub, but in a speedboat. It would be driven by the young manager himself.

"I hope you can swim," he shouted as we sped off down the river. He was gleeful, reckless – no doubt with relief at his temporary escape from the nightmare we had just witnessed.

117

"Why?" David, who had never been an enthusiastic swimmer, asked tentatively.

"In case we hit a crocodile." And, indeed, it seemed only too possible that any floating object struck at this speed would flip us over like a pancake.

It was as if, by changing boats, we had jumped into another epoch. Gone, the slow, gentle throb of the baleinière, the tranquillity of the water, the sensation of meandering through a green, watery maze of ever-lasting jungle. Now we were roaring, racing down an immensely complicated highway, carelessly churning up the water hyacinths and spitting them out in our wake. Palm trees, islands, fishing villages flashed past – visual images barely assimilated before they, too, were carelessly spat out in gobbets. At one stage, Charles let go of his comforter, the silk scarf from which he had never yet been parted. It flew away, was gone, left miles behind. No going back. The boat bumped and slapped into the wavelets. Dispelling the myths and the shadows with our modern technology, we were speeding into the very heart of darkness that I had read about.

Within a few hours, a column of smoke could be seen diffusing into the sky ahead of us. Then the factory chimneys, like tall reeds, detached themselves from the surrounding jungle.

"Look, look!" exclaimed Dr Kokou, who was as exhilarated by our dare-devil ride as the rest of us. "There's Elizabetha!"

Although small by European standards, it was by far the biggest land-mark we'd come across during our one-hundred-and-fifty-mile trip down-river from Stanleyville. As we got closer, we glimpsed some houses. They were scooped out of the greenery, tucked into the hillocks over-looking the river. I began to get more and more excited. I began, too, to be aware of the smell of boiling palm oil – something I'd get so used to that I'd stop noticing it – and to hear the thud, thud, thud of our own factory engines. We sped up to the beach. The boat was pulled ashore and we stepped out onto the wet sand. This was to be our own little outpost of the Empire.

Chapter 13

Within minutes of us arriving at our house in Elizabetha, there was a knock at the back door. I opened it to find a young man standing with a piece of paper in his hands.

"I am looking for work," he stated.

Although I didn't realise it at the time, our arrival had been heralded by the drums. "The new accountant," they said, "is a tall man and he wears glasses. His wife is young, but not so young. He has one boy-child and his wife is pregnant with another." I learned all this later from Nicholas, whom we decided to employ. Hearing the drums, he must have hurried straight round to our house, determined to be first.

David opened the testimonial that Nicholas handed him. I remembered these from my childhood: grubby pieces of paper taken in and out of pockets, folded so often that the creases started splitting apart. When I was little they had been written in flowery copperplate and invariably started with the words: "The bearer of this letter . . ." It had been the same in India and Africa. I retained a vivid sense of "the bearer of this letter". He'd always been nervous, sometimes even sweating and shaking. I'd known, because I must have been told, that a whole life was at stake; that without the job a family might starve. But I'd also known, though nobody had told me, that the writers of those letters were very ordinary people whose importance and power were often blown out of all proportion to their real worth.

David handed me the paper. This one was written in French and, quite apart from having to translate the formal, unfamiliar wording, I had already decided to take absolutely no notice of what it said. This time I was going to choose. I looked into Nicholas's eyes and knew that I liked him. David and I exchanged glances. Nicholas told us he could start straight away, so we employed him there and then. Within an hour, he had moved himself and his possessions into a hut at the back of the garden – screened from the house by a fence of palm fronds – and into my life.

Our house was one of those that we'd noticed as we'd approached the plantation. It was relatively new, but built in the colonial style with large, cool rooms that were fanned by the breezes that wafted through them. Perched on its own little hillock, it had a wide veranda where we could sit and look out across the river to the trees and the forest on the other side. Below us, there was a tangle of coffee plants scrambling down to the water. It was a view that would in time become so familiar it would become imprinted on my being.

What I hadn't realised to begin with was that Elizabetha was a mini-fiefdom. The Company had appropriated swathes of jungle the size of an English county to plant their rows and rows of palm trees. They were a huge industry, employing thousands of local workers and a dozen expatriates. Besides the main station, with its factories and offices, there were also substations. The nuts were grown, harvested and brought by the truckload to one or other of the factories to be loaded into huge vats, boiled and then pounded to extract the oil. The oil would be piped to tankers which then made their way down-river to Léopoldville. The labour force wasn't just needed to look after and harvest the fruit, roads had to be maintained and engines kept in working order.

As well as the European houses, which were dotted around at some distance from one another, there were African villages to house the workers. There was also a school, a hospital and a church – though I didn't learn of their existence for some time – a whole ministructure of a society. There was also a convent for the Catholic nuns who taught in the Company school, and a house for the priest who said Mass. The Company catered not only for the bodies of their workforce, but also their souls. The social centre was, predictably, the club, which was situated near the factory. But it was so modest, so informal, that there was no possibility of it being cliquey. There was a small brick building where it was possible to buy drinks, and there were a couple of tennis courts and a small swimming pool.

Our house was the furthest European house from the factory, so I didn't hear the pounding of the machines. David had been given his own car and he drove to and from the office. Within a very short time we settled into a routine. He would start work early at about six thirty, coming back for breakfast at about eight. We would sit on the veranda, with the early-morning sun gleaming on the river, eating papayas and lemon, and fresh rolls made by Nicholas. The coffee, probably because it was so absolutely fresh, was sublime, the best I would ever taste.

On our first morning, we were surprised by the sound of a child's soprano floating from the neighbouring hillock. I immediately recognised the tune, but it was so unexpected that it wasn't until a bar or so later that I realised they were singing their own uniquely African version of "Cwm Rhondda".

> Guide me, oh Thou great Jehovah,
> Pilgrim through this barren land . . .

It was too far away to hear the words, but the soprano had been joined by other voices, all harmonising till the rich echo of the full chorus reverberated over the little valley:

Bread of heaven, bread of heaven,

Feed me till I want no more . . .

These improbable harmonies were coming from a little church with open sides, and pillars to support a roof made of palm fronds. It looked just like the one in the film *The African Queen*.

Far from being a barren land, there was no shortage of food in Elizabetha. The small Company store sold most essentials. What meat there was, was cut up and shared out among the employees. Papayas and lemons grew fresh in the garden. Fish, tied in sheaves with string strung through their mouths, arrived straight from the river. The villagers sold us vegetables and eggs as well as skinny chickens. I hung a huge hand of bananas in the back veranda for anyone who passed to help themselves to, and felt munificent. As an added and unexpected bonus, Nicholas, our "boy", turned out to be a superb cook. He had been taught by the son of a Belgian restauranteur.

After Léopoldville, Elizabetha felt like paradise. But of course there had to be a snake in this Garden of Eden. No one in headquarters had thought to mention that David's predecessor had been beaten up. We were told the story by our new neighbour John Goodfellow, the chief engineer, a Devonshire man who'd been working in the Congo for several years. He called in to welcome us on our first evening.

"Their reasoning was frighteningly simplistic," he told us. "After Independence the new government announced a general pay rise. But when another government was instated after Lumumba's assassination, they retracted the order. Only, of course, nobody bothered to broadcast the fact. So a group of workers, convinced that they were owed more money, decided to pay a visit to the accountant's office. Although he tried to explain that the actual size of their wage packet had nothing to do with him, they laid into him. Luckily, he wasn't too badly injured. He lost a tooth; otherwise, it was mainly cuts and bruises."

John also broke it to us that, despite the medical facilities, there had been two white deaths on the plantation a few weeks previously. That was a shock, particularly since one of them had been a child, and there were very few European children in this part of the world. We were a hundred and fifty miles down-river from Stanleyville and over a thousand miles from distant Léopoldville, and in the case of a real emergency there was no real help to be had. It was something I couldn't even contemplate.

The extreme precariousness of our situation was brought home to me a few days later. We had just breakfasted in our own little piece of paradise, and David had left for the office again, when I heard a huge explosion that sounded like a land mine. David had sent the car back to the house with a driver, and he went straight into the kitchen, where I heard animated voices.

"What is it?" I asked.

"Un accident," Nicholas explained. It had apparently taken place at the factory. "Dix cadavres."

Ten corpses! "Vite," I said to the driver. "Quick. Take me to the factory straight away." I knew there were only two doctors, including Kokou, and presumably only a few nurses. I was pretty squeamish as far as blood was concerned, but I had cast myself as Florence Nightingale. As we sped along the bumpy dirt road I prepared myself for the scene of carnage. There would be corpses, of course, and blood lying in clotted pools, with severed feet and hands littering the floor. This would be my chance to prove my character. We got to the factory fast, but before we could go in we were stopped by two white men scurrying through the gates. Their faces were ashen. One of them tore open the car door and leapt in. He was followed by his companion. They squashed in beside me in the back, slamming the door shut.

"Vite!" one of them said to the driver in an English accent. "Au bureau!"

The driver slewed the car round and headed for the office.

"Thank God you came when you did," a young man with a dark curly beard and a Birmingham accent gasped. This wasn't part of my heroic rescue plan and I felt cheated.

"What about the accident?"

"It was the workers. They were after our blood," the other man, who was also English and even younger, panted.

"We were about to be lynched."

"What?"

"Christ, that was a near thing."

"But the corpses . . ."

"What corpses?"

Their words tumbled over each other in the hysteria of the moment.

"There's mayhem in there . . ."

"I tell you, they've gone mad."

It might have been tempting to dismiss the young engineers' account as melodrama, had I not been told about David's predecessor. I didn't begin to piece together the full story of what had happened at the factory, however, till David got home for lunch.

"The lid on one of the sterilising vats blew off," he told me. "They're the size of a room. And the boiling nuts were blasted out in all directions like red-hot bullets. The explosion was so powerful, the lid ended up in the river."

"What about the workers?"

"Mercifully, the men were having a tea break, so there weren't as many as usual around."

125

"The driver said there were ten corpses."

"No one seems to know exactly how many people were injured, but it sounds to me like a bit of an exaggeration. Fontaine called a meeting of the councillors at once to defuse the situation." Fontaine was the managing director, in general control of Elizabetha.

"'To defuse the situation'?" It seemed an understatement.

"He's given all the workers a day off and declared a public holiday for tomorrow."

As it happened, Fontaine, M le Directeur, had already invited us to dinner that evening to meet the other heads of department. John Goodfellow was among the guests. As he was responsible not only for the factory, but also for the two engineers I'd picked up so unceremoniously that morning, I heard the story first-hand.

"One of the workers apparently got so fed up with the hissing of the safety valve," he told me, "he took it into his head to jam it down. As the vats are rather like gigantic pressure cookers, it wasn't surprising that it eventually exploded."

"The injuries must have been horrendous."

"One man lost an eye," he told us, "but apart from that it was just burns."

"Surely the burns were serious, with all that fruit flying around?"

"The people here are very stoical," Dr Monge, who was also at the dinner party, explained. "They do not make a fuss."

"You must not think that this sort of thing happens every day," Fontaine interposed with old-fashioned courtesy.

M and Mme Fontaine were like the lord and lady of this little fiefdom and, as with anyone in authority, it was impossible not to feel a little in awe of them. He was a tall, proud man, and his wife ran her dinner party like an ambassadress. In spite of the fact that we were in the middle of the jungle, the polished table was laid with cut glass, starched table napkins and a couple of impressive silver candelabras. The wine had been decanted and the pâté de foie gras was already on little plates at our places. When it was time to eat we were all seated formally, according to rank. I was placed on our host's right. This, I presumed, was because of my husband's position. Known officially as M le Comptable, Mr Accountant was clearly high up in the pecking order.

Not surprisingly, the main topic of conversation was the accident. On our way to dinner we'd heard singing and dancing from one of the villages.

"That'll be the workers," John Goodfellow said. "They're having a party because they don't have to go to work tomorrow and they can afford to get drunk."

"What do they drink?"

"Palm wine. It's potent stuff. There'll be quite a few hangovers in the morning."

"But what about the men who were injured?"

"Oh, they'll be all right."

"But the man who lost an eye . . ."

"Alvarez-Montoya will get him a glass one." Alvarez-Montoya, I gathered, was the other doctor.

"He'll be able to show off about it," John went on, taking a swig of wine. "It'll single him out from the rest. You'll see, by the day after tomorrow the whole thing will be in the past."

"But they can't be so callous."

"It's not really callousness. More like fatalism. There was another accident when a man got his foot caught in the machinery. His friends carried him up to the doctor's surgery and, as it was rather bloody and mangled, they urged the doctor to cut it off."

"And did he?"

"No. He managed to save it. But they seem to take death and mutilation in their stride."

I couldn't help wondering if it was this people's history that had created their apparent devil-may-care attitude. These were after all the grand- and great-grandchildren of men who'd been brutalised during King Léopold's reign. Had the scars of the horror travelled down from generation to generation, or was brutality normal in human beings? Perhaps, I thought, people like me, who had never experienced war and violence first-hand, were oversensitive, too squeamish. And yet, there was no getting away from the fact that it took unimaginable brutishness to give orders to chain up slaves and amputate their hands. Perhaps that was why a certain type of white man dressed up in a dinner jacket every evening – to detach himself from the horror of his actions. Dining on sumptuous European wines and delicacies, he'd have made small talk about the "natives", while raking in the profits from their labours.

The party in the village was still going strong when we drove home. Fontaine, it seemed, had judged his workforce accurately. I went to sleep to the sound of drums, which throbbed like a heartbeat in my dreams.

Drums of a different sort – talking drums – soon became an integral part of my life. They pattered away at intervals, near and far, all through the day and night. Not that they were in any way intrusive. In fact, unless I made a conscious effort, I stopped noticing them. But they were there: a Morse code of news and gossip, people passing on messages, talking to one another. It was a world of which we were a part and yet to which we did not belong. It emphasised just how close we were to the spirit of the jungle, and at the same time how cut off from it.

Chapter 14

Elizabetha, I soon discovered, was a mini-United Nations. The engineers were all British, the two doctors Spanish, and most of the white managers were Belgian. They, in turn, were subdivided into the upper-class Walloons, who spoke French, and the Flamands, who spoke Flemish. The Walloons looked down on the Flamands as being inferior.

At M le Directeur's dinner, I'd realised that the Belgians were snobbish. In our tiny fiefdom, everything depended on the status of a person's job. This was brought home to me when I took Charles out for a walk. All the workers on the roads had doffed their caps, so to speak, and when I passed some mud huts, the women stopped pounding their manioc and stood up to greet me with a "Bonjour, Mme le Comptable", while the children, hiding behind their mother's skirts, had peeped round to get a look at Mrs Accountant as if I were royalty.

Having experienced the standoffishness of the Belgians in Léopold-ville, I was touched when, soon after our arrival, Mme Delvaux, M le Personnel's wife, invited us to dinner. She had been at M Fontaine's party, but we hadn't had a chance to speak. She wanted, she said, to introduce us to some friends. We arrived before the other guests. Although M Delvaux struck me as a rather colourless person, Madame was very smart. Her house was not only spick-and-span, it was luxuriously furnished. Even here, in the middle of the jungle, she kept up appearances. And she was proud of her cuisine. What wasn't imported was home-grown, she informed me. She had well-mannered chickens, which were kept out of the way in a pen and provided her with eggs. She also had a potager, a vegetable garden filled with exotic tropical fruit and vegetables. In addition, the Delvauxs had an eight-year-old daughter who, we were told, was very clever. And, most importantly, did her lessons, "correspondence", together with Mme le Directeur's son.

The friends she had invited us to meet were the mechanic and his wife. On the surface, it seemed an odd choice. M Verbruggen was in charge of maintaining the motor vehicles on the plantation. His wife, a Flemish housewife, spoke French with such a guttural accent it was almost impossible to understand her. Seated beside M le Mécanicien at the dining table, I struggled to find something to talk about. His main topic of conversation, interspersed with plenty of zuts and merdes, appeared to be the iniquities of les indigènes. Feeling battered myself by his abuse of his "native" workers, I tried to work out why on earth David and I had been chosen to meet these particular friends.

The Delvauxs had been in Elizabetha for quite a long time. As a Walloon, Madame clearly knew all about Belgian etiquette, which was why I was surprised to find myself seated not on her husband's right, but on M Delvaux's left. Being an outsider, I couldn't have cared less and certainly wasn't about to take umbrage at that sort of thing. But I knew that the Belgians did care. John Goodfellow had told me about one wife who'd been so insulted by not having her husband's job position properly recognised in the table seating that, as soon as she'd realised where she was being put, she'd got up and left the dinner party. I wondered whether Madame, assuming I was unaware of these things, was subtly trying to flatter Mme le Mécanicien. It seemed more likely, though, that she was getting her own back because she had been seated below me, on Fontaine's left, at the general manager's dinner party. Even though my French may not have been quite up to scratch, I was learning fast.

After dinner, Mme Delvaux told me all about her heart. Along with her position in society, this, I soon discovered, was her raison d'être.

"Angine," she said melodramatically, patting her chest.

"'Angine'?" I didn't know the word.

"Comme je souffre." I nodded sympathetically. This was clearly the right thing to do. She was always consulting the doctor, she said. Only the other day, her husband had been forced to call him up in the middle of the night. It wasn't until I got home and checked the dictionary that I realised she was suffering from angina.

It was Mme Delvaux who told me I had made a mistake in employing Nicholas. "He has a bad reputation," she told me.

"Why?"

"He drinks."

"Does he steal?"

"No," she said, she had not heard that he stole, but he was cheeky. It would have been wise, she said, to consult the other wives on the plantation before employing him.

I duly acknowledged this. But, really, I didn't care a damn about that lapse, any more than I cared about my perceived status. I liked Nicholas's cheek, if that was what it was. He said what he thought. It was true, he did drink, but only on his days off. We may not have had much in common with one another on the surface, but we instinctively understood one another. I also very soon realised that I would have been lost without him. It wasn't just that he got up early to clean the house. All the cooking was done on a primitive wood-burning stove, and the water had to be heated in a large metal container in the garden with a fire underneath it. Both had to be lit morning and evening, and the stove had to be carefully tended so that the naked flames didn't shoot up through the holes on the top. Meals would appear and hot water would come out of the taps, without my having to think about it. Nicholas also baby-sat whenever we went out.

One afternoon, while I was on my bed reading, I heard the high-pitched persistent cry of a baby coming from the direction of the back garden. As Charles was in his cot resting, I knew it couldn't be him. I got up to go and see where the noise was coming from, and found Nicholas pacing up and down the lawn at the back of the house with a screaming baby in his arms: the picture of a flustered father. He was full of apologies, presuming that he'd disturbed me. I assured him he hadn't and asked him what the matter was. It was his wife, he explained. She'd gone off to the market, leaving him to look after the baby. I'd had no idea that Nicholas had a wife, much less a baby. He looked far too young.

"Give her to me," I said. I knew it was a "her" because the baby was wearing a frilly dress. Nicholas handed over the quivering bundle. I took her in my arms. The baby gave a deep gasp, and then a shudder, and then stopped.

"Thank you."

That was the moment of our real bonding. Nicholas had adored Charles from the start, and Charles, in turn, had taken to him. Now his daughter had paid me the ultimate compliment of trusting me. As an ex-colonial, I felt particularly gratified. We agreed that, although Charles was older than little Stephanie, the children should play together. It was good for both of them. From then on, Charles frequently disappeared into the compound behind the palm fronds and returned smelling of manioc, the staple diet. He spoke his first word in Lingala. Although Nicholas was my servant, he was the first black man who'd become a really close friend.

Chapter 15

David and I settled down to what in many ways was a perfect life. Quite apart from the fact that we had Nicholas to make it so, the weather was warm, though never, in my memory, unbearably hot. Because we were relatively high up, there was always a breeze. David got up early and went to the office, coming back for breakfast and lunch. In the evenings, if we weren't going out or entertaining, David and I would read aloud to one another. We had brought a whole lot of classics with us, including Dickens, Thackeray, Jane Austen and Tolstoy. At ten o'clock the lights would go out. This was because the station generator, which was old and not very reliable, and frequently spluttered to a stop, was automatically turned off at night. After ten, we went to bed by candlelight. The rhythm suited both of us. Most days, Charles and I walked to the club for a swim, otherwise I'd sit on my veranda, reading or sewing. The river, the slow-moving mass of water that flowed across half a continent, became my life.

The big event of the week was the arrival of the tiny aeroplane. Charles and I would run out into the garden to watch it as it circled once round the plantation, like a huge bird, before landing on the airstrip on the other side of the river. The plane brought the mail, and a boat would be sent over from Elizabetha to collect it. Even more exciting was the paddle steamer that came all the way up-river from Léopoldville. Long before it made an appearance, its arrival would be announced by the distant sound of drums coming from somewhere down-river. Then, from far

133

away, we'd hear the chug of a paddle labouring its way against the current. As it got closer, crowds would gather down at the beach. We could hear the babble of voices, the mounting excitement. This was the villagers' one taste of the big city and a life so far away and so different as to be unimaginable. With the boat's actual arrival, the volume increased. There was a mounting hubbub as people fought to sell or buy. Women screamed as they tottered up the gangplank, backs loaded with babies, heads toppling with pots, or huge hands of bananas, or bunches of manioc leaves. After a while, above the din, we'd hear the voice of the Belgian captain over the Tannoy, "Attention! Attention!", as he tried to prepare for departure. At last he would win, and the boat would get going. Once again there was that beat of the paddle, this time getting fainter and fainter until gradually it faded into silence. After this brief visit, it felt as if the world had, once more, departed.

Although we didn't see a great deal of the other people during the week, at weekends we went to the club and swam and played tennis. And, inevitably, in a small community like ours, we got to know most of the other whites very well. There were so few of us that each became a quirky individual in their own right. I also began to learn how we were perceived by the Congolese people. Nicholas had by this stage become such a close friend that I didn't have to explain myself to him, he seemed to understand my mind. During one of our many conversations, he told me that all the white people were automatically given African names. What amazed me was how accurate they were. The inhabitants of the jungle had got us all worked out all right. M Fontaine was "the proud one", M Delvaux "the man who lets his wife rule", M le Mécanicien "the one who loses his temper". It was as if we were characters in their ongoing soap opera. Not surprisingly, Nicholas didn't tell me what David and I were called, but he did say that the person they most respected was given the name "salt". The name would have suited David.

In the meantime, each of us, cut off from our roots, was in our own way living out some sort of dream. This was particularly true of Dr Alvarez-Montoya, a Spaniard, whose English was excellent as he'd done his internship in Eastbourne. He worked at a lonely substation, so spent all his free time in Elizabetha. We'd already heard about him when we were in Léopoldville – like us, he had done his stint there. Besides being "a character", he'd gained a reputation as a ladies' man, leaving behind, so it was said, a trail of hungry wives and desolate daughters. Although there were very few wives and no nubile daughters in Elizabetha, he didn't mind because there were other compensations.

Alvarez-Montoya's burning ambition was to become a plastic surgeon. In Eastbourne he'd had the opportunity of working with one and it had been love at first cut. Although as yet unqualified, he had come to the Congo to satisfy a deep yearning to remould the human body. Rumour had it that Mme Bossart had allowed him to lift her forty-year-old breasts – presumably as a lure for the smitten Mr Wilkinson – but Léopoldville offered limited opportunities. Here at Elizabetha, however, Dr Alvarez-Montoya had a whole jungle full of people at his disposal. He was continually on the lookout for patients who might want bits of their anatomy enhanced.

One of his victims had apparently been the ball boy at the club. The lad had a lazy eye. After a short spell in hospital, the ball boy reappeared on the tennis court with both eyes wide open. It was said, though, that at night he could no longer close the one that had been operated on. Whether or not this was true, it was also said that after the operation the workers ran away whenever they saw "Monsieur le Médecin" looking at them speculatively.

Alvarez-Montoya had probably told this story against himself. He was generally loved for his high spirits and sense of the ridiculous. Everyone felt free to make jokes about him while he in turn enjoyed ribbing other people, particularly a young bachelor, Dick Meekings. Dick was one of the engineers I had picked up outside the factory gates after the sterilising vat had exploded. Although he'd only just left university, he had grown a beard and assumed an air of gravitas. As well as taking himself seriously, Dick had a yearning to be someone different. He shared a house with the other young engineer, Keith, and would sit on the veranda in a paisley dressing gown, smoking a pipe and reading *Argosy* and *Blackwood's Magazine*, and looking every bit the Somerset Maugham-type character he aspired to.

Dick was also building a car. It had been sent out to the Congo in kit form and was supposed to end up as a sports car. No one believed that it would ever be finished, much less take to the road.

"I would not like to be one of your passengers," Alvarez-Montoya ribbed, "unless I took out a special insurance." That was also a running joke. Dick didn't believe in insurance.

The drums, Nicholas had told me, called Dick "the man who does not like to part with his money" – and they were right. "I've got better things to spend my money on," he'd boasted when David suggested he insure his belongings. "And anyway, I've always got Tookey." Tookey was a fox terrier that Dick had brought out with him from England. "Good guard dog," he would say importantly as the animal yapped at anyone who came near. "No one would dare rob me." He didn't believe in banks either, and would boast that he kept his savings in a secret hiding place in the house.

"You are a typical Englishman," Alvarez-Montoya would tease. "You love your dog more than you will ever love any woman."

"Nonsense," Dick spluttered.

"On the other hand . . ." Alvarez-Montoya put on an air of seriousness. "Have I told you? The baby has started to grow a beard . . ."

This was an allusion to another running joke. From time to time, half-caste babies would be born to black mothers in the village. The Company took the paternity of these babies seriously. The mother was asked to name the father, who was then forced to pay a maintenance allowance for his child. After the most recent birth, rumour had it, the mother had given a list of four possible white fathers out of a total of twelve white males on the plantation. The rumour could well have been perpetrated by Alvarez-Montoya himself. Though he would never have broken his oath of secrecy, he had told Dick that one of the names on the list was his.

"You can't say things like that," Dick, though probably flattered, had protested. "I'll have you up for libel."

The other doctor on the plantation, Monge, was completely different. Where Alvarez-Montoya came from sophisticated Barcelona, Monge came from Andalusia. Alvarez-Montoya was fair, Monge was dark. His black hair grew low on his forehead, which gave him a saturnine look. He was well built, stocky and in his early forties. He had no English banter. In fact, he said very little. He had been working on the plantation for several years and appeared to regard Elizabetha as home. His was a busy life, for, besides seeing patients in his clinic, he ran the local hospital. Everyone I talked to respected him, held him in awe even, both as a man and a doctor. It was one of the things people clung to. The faith that, whatever happened to them, Monge would somehow cope.

One of the two European deaths had, I discovered, happened while Monge was away on leave. But Alvarez-Montoya wasn't to blame. When the young man, an assistant electrician, had come to the clinic with a pain in his stomach, Alvarez-Montoya had diagnosed appendicitis and told him that he would have to have an operation straight away.

"I'm not going to let you butcher me about," the young man was reputed to have said. He'd been due to go on leave in the next day or two and was determined to wait till he got back to Europe. He'd then gone home, climbed into a hot bath and the pain had, miraculously, gone away. This, it soon transpired, was because his appendix had burst. But the subsequent emergency operation, probably after septicaemia had set in, had by all accounts been successful. Alvarez-Montoya was a good surgeon and the young man had come round in high spirits. When his wife and friends had visited the patient, he'd been sitting up in bed with a drain sticking out of his abdomen, cracking jokes. Soon after they left, however, he'd keeled over and died. Postoperative shock was the diagnosis.

"It wasn't the doctor's fault," people said. But they also said: "Monge would not have allowed it. He would have insisted on the operation." Alvarez-Montoya, still rather raw, had simply offered a serious warning. But he must have felt that he was to blame. It was a heavy burden to carry so early on in his career. To make matters worse, the young man had left a widow who had been flown back to Brussels. She was pregnant with their first baby.

Chapter 16

Although I was very fond of Alvarez-Montoya – it was impossible not to be, he was such an open, generous character – it was Monge who really fascinated me. I was drawn to his taciturn nature. He was an enigma. Although I'd met him briefly at the Fontaines' dinner party and had seen him when I'd gone for my antenatal checkups, I hadn't spoken to him properly as a person until a Company party that was held at the club one Sunday lunchtime. Everyone had been asked to bring something to eat, and Monge had produced a platter of little pizzas. When I told him how delicious they were, he said he would teach me how to make them. I accepted the invitation, not, I admit, because I was desperate to learn how to make Spanish pizzas, but because I was curious to find out more about his domestic setup. For I had heard Monge was living openly with a Congolese woman. Rumour had it that she was in fact the second of his common-law wives, and that both women had borne him children.

There was no one else around when I arrived at Monge's house, not even a servant. We had the kitchen – which was even more primitive than my own – entirely to ourselves. Monge, who took the making of pizzas extremely seriously, handled the wood-burning stove like an expert. He had all the pizza ingredients laid out and ready for me. He'd already made the dough, which had been left to rise, and kept saying "encore de l'huile" as he sloshed in more and more olive oil while kneading with the palm of his thick hand. By the time they went into the oven, the pizzas were so saturated they were oozing oil.

After we had finished the cooking, Monge offered me a cup of tea. In order to get a snoop around his house, I asked for the bathroom. There were no signs of a wife, and the only evidence of her possible existence was a large double bed shrouded by a mosquito net. The other bedroom was far too tidy to be a children's room. I came to the conclusion that Monge's Congolese "wife" – if indeed she existed – lived in the village and only visited him at night. Although it was a romantic idea, it was also a little disappointing. One of the things I'd admired about Monge was his directness, his lack of hypocrisy. I'd have liked him to flaunt a black wife. For although on the plantation there was no opprobrium attached to sleeping with a black woman, most men kept their peccadilloes under wraps.

This was a good deal more liberal than Rhodesia, where sleeping with a black woman had been, outwardly at any rate, unthinkable. In South Africa it was illegal. Here, with the wives away, it was commonplace – M le Mécanicien's van was, I'd been told, frequently seen lurking in the village in the afternoons when the men were all at work. There was, however, one European man who had turned completely "bush", as we would have said in Rhodesia. We met him when we took the motorised canoe to the village on the other side of the river.

I had recently managed to acquire a brand-new sewing machine. The Company had had a consignment of twelve, which it sold to us cheaply at the official rate of exchange. It was the old-fashioned manual kind, like the one my mother had used in Rhodesia, and meant I could make clothes for the baby. As the Company boat went across the river from time to time, we decided to go on a shopping spree to buy material to make baby clothes. Basoko was an old trading post with a historic fort, but its real centre was the store, which was run by a Portuguese trader. It was the only place for hundreds of miles around where one could buy anything apart from food. The shop, a large barn of a room, must have been a kind of Mecca for locals. Sacks of beans jostled for space with brightly painted enamel bowls, and bales of hessian stood side by side with Jeyes Fluid. It was a jungle superstore selling everything from food to printed cottons and beads. The cotton was a bit rough, but I managed to find some handmade lace for the baby's dresses.

The trader's living quarters appeared to be an extension of the store, and at one stage a woman came through to the shop. From the familiar and easy way she treated him, it was obvious that the trader was her lover, especially as the child who was balanced on her hip was pale-skinned. In fact, looking round and into the room beyond, and seeing other children of varying ages who were also the colour of milky coffee, I realised there were several of his offspring. The trader was a great deal older than his mistress. She was young, but she was proud. She wasn't going to kowtow to anybody. Tall and beautiful, she carried herself with dignity. We were not that far from Rwanda-Burundi, and I decided that she must be a Tutsi.

Although the trader was in his late middle age and had deteriorated physically – his belly flopped over the belt of his shorts, his hair was completely unkempt, and his teeth were in a terrible state – there was something about him that was attractive. And even if he did seem old, he would have been a good catch simply by virtue of his colour. Besides that, the ownership of a store in this part of the world would have made him a millionaire in Congolese francs.

As in the case of Monge, I was fascinated that such things could happen. That black and white could live together. In the brave new world of independent Africa, I had not thought about people of different colours marrying one another. It wasn't that I had any moral objections, but I was still stuck in the mindset of my upbringing.

141

When David's London boss came out to the plantation on tour, we invited Edward, David's black accounts assistant, to Sunday lunch to meet him. He was a Ghanaian. In the newly liberated world of the 1960s, with Prime Minister Harold Macmillan's "wind of change" speech blowing through Africa, the Company had imported a token number of black managers. In Elizabetha, one of these was a Congolese citizen, but the other two were Ghanaian. As a manager, Edward had been allowed to bring his family to the Congo with him, so naturally we also invited his wife and two children to lunch.

I had never entertained black people before, and I wondered how Nicholas would react to this. He was enthusiastic and suggested we serve them traditional Congolese mwambe, particularly in view of the fact that some of our guests were foreigners. His version was a chicken dish with palm oil and chillies, accompanied by rice and manioc leaves.

Our visitors arrived in their Sunday best. But, where David and the London financial director were dressed casually in short-sleeved shirts, Edward was wearing a suit and a stiff collar. In a spirit of male camaraderie, the white men urged him to take off his jacket and tie. He was awkward and slightly embarrassed – these men were after all his seniors – but he did it. As far as his wife Stella was concerned, it was impossible to get her to loosen up. Her dress seemed to be made of an excessively hot nylon fabric, and she wore stockings. Her little boy, a couple of years older than Charles, had been dressed up in a miniature suit with a bow tie. The baby girl was in pink frills.

I liked Edward. He had a round face with pebble-thick glasses, and I soon realised that, unlike Mr Wilkinson, or indeed David, he had taken a degree. Spotting *Great Expectations* on the table, he told me that at Accra University, where he'd studied accounting, he'd also developed a taste for Dickens.

"I can understand Pip," he said. "I also left my traditional home to make my way in the big city. Even though I did not have any great expectations, I think in many ways I am like him. In my heart I am still a country boy."

"And I am a bit like Mrs Pocket," I said.

"Mrs Pocket?"

"She was Pip's friend's mother. She was always reading books and she left her children to grow up by themselves, to 'tumble up'."

Edward laughed.

"The family lived beside the Thames, and I was always afraid that one of her babies would tumble into the river."

"In my culture it is hard to imagine children being left alone. There are always plenty of women in Ghana. Plenty of relatives. If one woman cannot care for her child, another will look after him. Although, these things are beginning to change," he added.

"Why?"

"For many reasons. It is partly cultural, but it is also urbanisation."

"That's a shame."

"You cannot stop progress."

"Have another beer." David had come across the room to join us, before steering Edward away from me. I should have liked to have gone on talking to him, but the financial director was, after all, the reason for the invitation. And the men needed to talk business.

In contrast to her husband, Stella was difficult to engage in conversation. Although she spoke English, she only answered "yes" or "no" to the questions I asked her. She was too shy to elaborate. Her small son was equally inhibited. While Charles ran around the room, the little boy sat bolt upright on the sofa, drinking Fanta.

It was inevitably a tense situation. David talked shop with Edward, while the financial director was overjolly and slightly flirtatious with Stella. I was worried about everything, including the meal. Even Nicholas was trying too hard. The only person who appeared completely unfazed by the situation was the baby. She was about eighteen months old, a bright little girl who scuttled around on the floor attempting to get onto and into anything she could, and creating a welcome diversion. Then, just as we were about to eat, she started to cry. Stella picked her up and, sitting on the sofa, started to suckle her. I wasn't sure whether to delay the lunch, or go ahead. As it happened, within minutes the child was asleep and we were able to get on with our meal.

"You must come to tea with me," I said to Stella when it was time to say goodbye. It wasn't only that I felt that, as the boss's wife, I should do something. I was certain that, away from the men, she would be forthcoming.

She smiled politely and said, "Thank you."

"How charmingly uninhibited these people are," the financial director remarked after Edward and his family had left, presumably referring to the breast-feeding. What he didn't remark on – what none of us remarked on – was that each of the two children appeared to have a different father. The older child was very dark, the younger much, much paler, almost white. Edward had, I knew, worked on another of the Company plantations. Stella was very pretty. I couldn't help wondering if there had been vans lurking around *her* house in the afternoons.

No one could have condemned Stella. From what I'd observed, I didn't imagine an African woman had much choice if a white man took it into his head to sleep with her. But I felt very sorry for Edward. Most cuckolded husbands don't have to live with proof of their wives' infidelity, but in his case the child's colour appeared to be a giveaway.

Chapter 17

I was sitting on my veranda one morning, sewing a garment for the new baby, due in a couple of months' time, when I became aware of screams coming from the back of the house. I hurried through the kitchen to find a woman holding a naked baby under the outside tap with its big stone basin where Nicholas did the washing. She was dangling the child upside down by its ankles while at the same time blowing water into its mouth. The child was not only screaming, it was writhing in indignation. At the first opportunity, it tried to lift its head, and yelled. That was when I realised it was Nicholas's daughter, Stephanie.

"What are you doing?" I asked urgently. It looked as if the woman was trying to drown the child.

The woman, who didn't hear me, took another mouthful of water from the tap and, clamping her mouth to the baby's, blew the tap water into the baby's mouth. A stream of snot poured out of its nose and I realised that she was irrigating its nasal system. The convulsing body tried once more to lift its head and scream. It was only then that the woman looked up and saw me. She stopped and looked at me in alarm.

"What are you doing?" I repeated. Clearly, Nicholas's wife – for I'd worked out that that was who she must be – didn't understand what I was saying. She seemed to think that I was querying her use of the basin.

"It's not that," I said, feeling awkward because I couldn't communicate. "I was worried about the baby." She didn't say anything. I glanced around to see if Nicholas was anywhere to be seen so that he could explain. But he seemed to have gone out. Then his wife took Stephanie in her arms and hurried back to her hut behind the palm fronds.

The incident made me feel uneasy on several counts. Part of me worried about the procedure; whether it was right to blow water through a child's nasal system – though presumably, hanging upside down, Stephanie couldn't actually drown. The other part worried whether I should have interfered at all. I wondered, then, what went on when Charles played with Stephanie in Nicholas's hut. Nothing dangerous, I was sure, because Nicholas was always – or nearly always – there. I also felt bad that I hadn't even recognised Nicholas's wife. I was reminded of the time in Rhodesia when I hadn't recognised our own houseboy's face. Despite the fact that the woman lived in my back garden, she had simply been a figure occasionally glimpsed, but no more. It wasn't just that she spoke no French; she was a rural peasant.

What the incident brought home to me was that we lived in separate worlds, and that Nicholas wanted to keep it that way. To me, he was a sensitive, intelligent human being. But he was also a man and a chauvinist. "Your baby will be a boy," he would say, as if that were the only gender worth giving birth to. He straddled the cultures. A husband, a father and, doubtless, an autocrat in his own home; a servant, as well as a gentle friend, in mine. He loved Charles as if he were his own son. On one occasion, when David and I went to lunch with John Goodfellow, there was a sudden thunderstorm in the middle of the meal. Worrying that Charles, whom I'd left at home asleep in his cot, might wake up and be frightened, I hurried home. I got back to the house to find Nicholas had had the same thought. He was crouched outside Charles's room. I couldn't help wondering whether he'd have done the same for his daughter.

The incident served to remind me how little I knew of the black world out there. One of the reasons I'd been excited about coming to the Congo was that I'd hoped to get a chance to get a feel of that other world. I'd wanted to integrate, to understand. That was why I asked David's driver – he used to come to take me shopping, just as George had done – if he would take me to the local Congolese market. None of the other Europeans on the plantation had been there, and when I asked them why, they said there was nothing to buy. The driver seemed surprised, but took me all the same.

It turned out to be much like most African markets. There was a large clearing where the vendors – all women – sat with their wares on woven palm mats, while buyers wandered around, stopping to look or haggle over the price. It was true that there wasn't much to buy. No barrow loads of fruit and vegetables, no colourful African ambiance. The women sat with small heaps of dried fish and bundles of strange herbs, as well as manioc roots and leaves piled on the dusty earth. Familiar vegetables like lettuce and tomatoes and beans were of poor quality. Flies buzzed and hovered everywhere, particularly over the fish. The women continually brushed them away with fans made of woven palm leaves. I felt out of place. Not that anyone was deliberately rude, but I knew I was intruding. None of them tried to sell me their wares and I got the feeling that I had somehow trespassed.

As I was leaving, I saw Stella. There was a row of brick houses beside the market and she was standing outside one of these, chatting with a neighbour. She was dressed in a piece of African cloth which was wrapped round her body. Her baby was tied to her back in the traditional way. She looked far more comfortable than she had in her tight nylon dress. At first she didn't see me, or at least that's what I assumed. She was engrossed in conversation with a woman I presumed to be the other Ghanaian wife. My first reaction was surprise at seeing her in that place. Although I'd asked Stella to tea, I hadn't thought about where she might live. The villagers weren't only a different nationality, they were of a different class from Edward and Stella altogether.

"Hello, Stella," I called out, relieved to see a familiar face.

She looked up from her conversation, and for a moment I saw an expression of fear, almost panic, on her face. Then, like a schoolgirl who'd been caught out by a parent, she was flooded with embarrassment. She pulled her little boy to her and told him to greet me. It was as if she were ashamed of being seen dressed as she was and living in these surroundings, as if she'd been caught in her curlers.

"I've just been to the market," I said in what I knew must sound a falsely cheerful voice. I was hoping that Stella would introduce me to her friend. Although she'd been talking in a language I didn't understand, I'd have liked to have joined in on the conversation, been invited into her house, even. But there was clearly no question of that. This time, I was the one who was in the wrong environment.

My meeting with Stella made me conscious of being part of a collective doublethink. In one sense we regarded these people as savages, and in another as the people of tomorrow. One Sunday, a black man came to the club with some children. He was an elderly man and the children may have been his grandchildren. He looked unworldly, and I would have put him as a pastor. His children, like Edward's family at our lunch party, were dressed in their best European clothes for the occasion. Although these were beautifully washed and ironed and even starched, they were a mishmash that included a pair of pyjama bottoms; the sort of clothing my family had given away to the servants.

Although there was no reason why the man and his family should not have been there – there was no official colour bar in the newly independent Congo – this was the first time I had seen a black person as a guest at the club. It was as if, just as I had done in the market, he were breaching some sort of bastion. No one reacted as the man came up to the bar and ordered drinks – a beer for himself, Fantas for the children – but nor did anyone greet him or talk to him. The man took his drinks back to the table where his family was seated.

I felt embarrassed for them. The little girls' hair was so beautifully parted and plaited, the little boys' faces so shiningly clean. They sat there, those children, feet dangling from the chairs, rubbing their skinny little legs together like cicadas, and sipping their expensive soft drinks. And suddenly I wanted to tell them that it wasn't worth it; that we weren't worth copying. I wanted my Africans to be noble savages, not ersatz Europeans. I wanted them to create their own world, their own unsullied civilisation, not emulate ours.

Was this to be our legacy? I thought angrily. Old clothes and sugary drinks?

I was reminded of a man I'd once seen as a schoolgirl. I was on the way to boarding school and our train stopped at a siding. There was a man working on the railway lines. He stopped and stood up. He was young and very tall. One of the girls threw a sandwich at him – it was a long journey, and our parents always gave us more than we could eat – and he caught it and ate it in one go. He was probably hungry. But then the other girls started throwing their sandwiches as well. He ate them all. It had become a game. I worried about what all that white bread was doing to his perfect teeth. It also struck me that he was probably somebody's husband and father, and that we were treating him like a performing dog.

Nobody was throwing sandwiches now, but the feeling was the same. The unexpected visitors to our club were not so much people as a spectacle. A joke. I could just imagine the dinner-party conversation: "Do you know, the old man was dressed in a hand-me-down suit and a plastic trilby!"

Chapter 18

One of the things I'd asked the financial director during his visit to Elizabetha was whether he didn't think it'd be a good idea for me to go back to England to have my baby. It wasn't that I was worried about giving birth on the plantation. Like everybody else, I had complete faith in Monge. But my brother, who was working at the time as a district commissioner in relatively nearby Northern Rhodesia, had written and suggested that I should consider going to stay with him. "Everyone here is worried about what's happening in your part of the world," he'd said. "There's a small hospital close by where you could have the baby." I was seven months pregnant, so if I were going to give birth elsewhere, I had to make the decision straight away. In a couple of weeks I wouldn't be allowed to travel.

The financial director dismissed my misgivings.

"There's absolutely nothing to worry about," he assured me. "If there were any serious trouble, the Company would be the first to know about it." He was not alone in his confidence. The United Nations had decided to withdraw some of their troops from the Haut-Congo, which surely meant that they did not foresee any serious trouble.

"And besides," the director added, "if you were to go home the Company couldn't send you back here, you know."

That determined it. I certainly wasn't going to leave David. We were both happy in Elizabetha. I had got the gardener to dig a potager and had taken to gardening myself. We were already harvesting our first radishes.

Also, as there was a ready-made pen behind the servants' quarters, we had acquired some chickens. They came from the market, so were pretty scrawny and didn't seem able to lay, but I was confident that in time they would provide us with eggs. By now I had written another article for the BBC and was planning a third after the birth. I would call it "Bush Baby".

Monge, who was a Catholic, had taken me round the hospital and introduced me to the nuns who would nurse me through my confinement. Many of the African mothers still gave birth, as they always had, in their villages, but where there was a threat of complications they were brought into the hospital. The maternity ward was a large open-sided room, like a veranda, with the roof held up by pillars. It was known as La Maternité.

Outside the ward, there was apparent chaos. Chickens pecked in the dirt while small children ran around or played in the dust. Visiting relatives squatted by small, home-made fires, cooking. Women in various stages of pregnancy sat on the steps or lolled against pillars, fanning themselves against the bluebottles. They were waiting, Monge told me, for their consultation at the antenatal clinic. Inside, the mothers who had just given birth lay on bedrolls on the concrete floor, their newborn babies beside them. With their little black milky mouths and coarse curls they seemed much tougher and better formed, more able to tackle the world they'd arrived in, than European babies. Only the soles of their feet and the palms of their hands were pink and seemingly vulnerable.

Although it would have been a novel experience – and made good copy for "Bush Baby." – Monge assured me that I would not be expected to give birth on a bedroll on a concrete floor. He introduced me to Sister Maria, the nun who would be my midwife. She took me to the European section of the hospital, a small brick bungalow, where I would have the baby in comparative luxury. There were only two wards – one for men and the other for women – and each had only one bed. Clearly, no one envisaged an epidemic breaking out in the European community. The room was simple and clean, with large windows and a grass lawn of sorts outside where Charles would be able to play. My bush baby was going to have a perfect introduction to the world.

After showing me the hospital, Sister Maria invited me back to the convent for tea. The nuns lived in what must have been a small replica of the Belgian nunnery from which they'd been sent. Tranquil, with bare whitewashed walls and simple, solid, gleaming wooden furniture, it reminded me of the film *The Nun's Story*. I'd always had a pretty clichéd view of nuns, picturing them living a sterile existence, but these were full of fun. And although the majority were white, there were also a couple of black sisters. They all appeared to mix quite happily together.

The nuns, who were as excited about the birth as I was, told me that they were already praying for me and my baby. They even invited me to a special celebratory tea.

"It is for Sister Bernadette," I was told. "This morning we got news that her father had died."

"Isn't she sad?" I asked. Sister Bernadette, who had a naturally merry disposition, was as full of smiles as any of them.

"Oh, no. It was his time. She is happy for him because he is with our Father in heaven." It seemed a sensible attitude towards old age and mortality. And, although I was a bit sceptical about their naïve faith, I liked the idea of being prayed for. It made me feel special and, I have to admit, safe.

Nicholas was also excited about the impending birth. "You are destined to be a mother of sons," he told me, as if he too had a hotline to the Almighty. And although I would have preferred a girl, I didn't dare say so.

So I sat on my veranda, embroidering pieces of white cotton cut from

David's old shirts, serenely confident that the birth of my baby was going to be without complications.

There was only one niggle. I hadn't entirely thrown off the fearfulness that had been imprinted on my nervous system in Léopoldville. Although I no longer had full-blown claustrophobia, and, although I was getting better at suppressing it, I was still prone to panic attacks. I couldn't altogether ignore the fact that here, in the middle of the jungle, we were very vulnerable.

The view from my veranda was beautiful. And it was always changing. Up here, a thousand miles from Léopoldville, the water drifted as if it had all the time in the world to get to the sea. When the sun shone it sparkled, when a storm was brewing it dully brooded. And occasionally, a coloured bird would emerge from the tangle of bushes.

The only blot on the view was a row of dead trees. They had been killed by the rise in the water level caused by the invasion of the water hyacinths. On my more anxious days, the leafless skeletons seemed symbolic. They reminded me of my own, as well as my small son and unborn baby's, mortality. This part of the world was, I knew, particularly dangerous for children. The trees were a reminder that if they got seriously ill, they had very little chance of survival.

I was haunted by the story of the little girl who'd died only weeks before we got to Elizabetha. She'd been the daughter of a missionary couple who lived on a station twenty miles up-river from Elizabetha, and she'd been the same age as Charles. The missionaries came down to the plantation about once a fortnight to collect their mail and buy whatever they needed from the Company store. It also enabled them to have some sort of contact with people outside of the missionary compound. Their only form of transport, however, was a motorised canoe.

The wives took it in turns to accompany whichever of the men was visiting the plantation and, when they discovered that there was an Englishwoman in Elizabetha, they came and had coffee or lunch with me. Because I was an outsider, the missionary wives felt able to talk more openly and frankly than they would have to one another. The death of the baby was one of their chief topics of conversation.

As it happened, the father of the little girl had arranged to go to Elizabetha just before the death occurred. She'd caught measles but her mother, who was a nurse, had not been particularly worried about her. While her father was away, however, the baby had developed a high fever. The measles had turned into pneumonia. Amazingly, the mission station had no radio contact with the plantation, and the mother of the sick child had had to sit it out in agony until her husband returned. The journey took about two hours each way, so it was eight hours before the father got home again from his trip. By that time the baby was seriously ill. They then put her into the boat and motored back in the dark to Elizabetha. The journey in a pirogue with a tiny engine must have felt endless. She'd still been alive when they arrived. But she hadn't survived the night.

Each of the missionary wives I met had a slightly different take on the tragedy.

"The trouble with Elspeth," one Dutchwoman told me in her no-nonsense fashion, "is that she is too proud. Just because she's a trained nurse she always thinks she knows better than any of us." She didn't actually say it was God's punishment, but that was the implication. It was a Protestant mission station, and hers was a harsh version of Christianity.

When I eventually met Elspeth, she was still, predictably, distraught.

"If only I'd taken her that morning . . . but she seemed perfectly well . . . I should have known . . ." Just talking about the baby brought on inconsolable bouts of tears. She had clearly lived and relived every moment of that fateful day, unable to forgive herself or find any comfort.

154

"Didn't you have any antibiotics?" That was something I hadn't been able to understand.

"I'd brought some with me," she said. "I always do. But I'd already used them all up." Being a nurse, it was she, of course, who was in charge of the health of the people who came to the mission station. She would have dished out antibiotics to whoever needed them. "I hadn't had the chance to replace them. There's always so much to do . . . so many people to see . . . In fact, they were on the list. I'd asked my husband to bring some back that day." Her face was white and ugly with grief.

"Are you thinking of having another baby?" I asked tentatively, aware of how painful to her the sight of my child as well as my pregnancy must be.

"We've tried, but nothing has happened . . . Perhaps this is my punishment . . . Perhaps God is angry with me . . . I know that I should believe that everything is for the best, but . . ." Her shoulders shook and shook as she tried to shed her burden of guilt.

I wondered who she talked to on the mission station and whether she was aware of what the other wives were saying behind her back. They seemed unnecessarily cruel and judgemental.

In contrast, the Roman Catholic nuns took a completely different view.

"She was a wonderful little girl," the sister who had nursed the baby told me. "Such a beautiful child. Eleven months old. And such spirit. She was brought to the hospital in the evening. We gave her antibiotics and she fought all through the night. I thought at one stage we might save her, but in the morning she died. We still pray for her soul. And for her mother, of course. Ah, la pauvre maman! The loss of a child is a terrible burden for any woman to bear."

The Catholics, I had discovered, were altogether more pragmatic and accepting in their faith. They took people as they found them. The black postulants were not expected to be virgins when they joined the order. And the one and only brother on the plantation lived in clover. He not only had a well-stocked wine cellar, he kept a cow and had the best potager on the plantation.

Jennifer, the youngest of the missionary wives, confirmed my impression of the Protestant mission being an isolated community of bitter, inward-looking souls. She had fairly recently got married and was pregnant with her first child.

"They were okay to begin with," she told me, "but once they realised I wasn't particularly religious, that was it. I wasn't one of them. The trouble is that it's not as if my husband is that hooked on religion either. I mean, Chris believes in God and wants to do good, but he's not one of them. He came out here for the experience. He volunteered to do a year's teaching." Genuine missionary material was, even by the early Sixties, running out.

"It's their idealism I can't handle," she went on. "It's so narrow-minded. So puritanical. Things are either good or bad. There's no compromise. No in-between."

One of the things that really worried Jennifer was that the missionaries insisted on changing everyone's money at the official rate of exchange. As Jennifer pointed out, this didn't help anybody: "It's only lining the pocket of some official or other."

She was right. The Catholics had no such scruples about playing the black market. David was continually carrying out currency transactions for them, and I said I'd ask him to change her money for her at the proper rate.

It was Jennifer who kept me reasonably au fait with what was happening in the outside world and what was going on in the Haut-Congo. She had sensibly brought with her a short-wave radio and was able to

156

pick up a crackly version of the BBC. There were more troubles in Haut-Congo, she told me, and they were not far from us. Also, the rebels had resurfaced in Northern Katanga and in the Kivu district on the border with Rwanda-Burundi. She painted a troubling picture and I couldn't help feeling apprehensive. The pockets of insurgence seemed like blisters on a hot asphalt road. They were erupting all around us.

"The young men are taking drugs and going to witch doctors," she said. "They've been told that if they smear themselves with magic grease, the enemy bullets will pass through them like water. Then they dress themselves in feathers and skins, and the local people are so terrified they simply cave in." These were the Simbas, whom Thoby had told us about in Léopoldville. At the time, the story had seemed fantastical, but now it was more difficult to dismiss.

"What about the United Nations?" I asked Jennifer. "There were plenty of them in Léopoldville, and they didn't seem to have much to do."

"Apparently they went in to liberate Albertville in the Kivu district when the town was taken over by the rebels," she said, "and they did manage to put down the rebellion. But it's like throwing water on a bush fire. It just flares up again somewhere else."

Jennifer, who was in the early stages of her pregnancy, said she'd definitely be going back home to have her baby.

That evening I told David what Jennifer had said, and asked him if he thought we should be worrying.

"It's just a bit of local trouble," he said, dismissing her stories as scaremongering. "The Company has its ear to the ground." Although it did occur to me that David knew more and that he was protecting me, I wanted – I needed – to believe that everything was going to be all right.

Chapter 19

The fact that the Company was clearly not too concerned about the troubles was confirmed when several women, including John Goodfellow's wife, arrived on the plantation. It was the start of the school holidays and now, whenever Charles and I went to the club, the swimming pool was full of splashing and laughter. One of the children was Mme Fontaine's older son. He attended a boarding school in Belgium where, at the end of the holidays, he'd be joined by his younger brother. Mme Delvaux's daughter would also be going to boarding school after the summer holidays. While the two wives sat beside the pool in the sunshine, talking about schools and uniforms, their children "bombed" the baths, splashing noisily as they jumped into the water clutching their knees.

There were also two new brides. One belonged to Keith, the young engineer. He'd told us before that he had a fiancée in Swindon and that he was planning to marry her and bring her back with him to Elizabetha. He looked so young, barely out of school, that I hadn't believed him. Neither had Alvarez-Montoya. When Keith had gone on leave, he took with him some chillies to give his wife-to-be a taste of the life to come.

"Are you planning to eat them before or after?" Alvarez-Montoya had ribbed. Chillies were considered something of a virility symbol among the white men in Elizabetha. To eat one whole proved that you were a "real man".

"They're not for me." Unlike Dick, Keith never rose to Alvarez-Montoya's bait. "I thought my fiancée might like to taste them. To see what sort of food she'd be eating out here."

"Aren't they more likely to act as a deterrent?" I joked.

"I don't think so." Keith delivered his lines in a calm West Country burr. "She's already made up her mind."

Life for the unmarried men was lonely on the plantation and I had taken Keith's certainty as wishful thinking. But he duly came back from his leave with an exceptionally pretty bride called Lorraine. She was diminutive, the sort of girl you would have thought couldn't possibly have survived outside her native Wiltshire. That, however, was on the surface. She turned out to have guts and a sense of humour. And she was mistress of the throwaway line. When I asked her what she thought of the chillies, she said she hadn't been given the chance to taste them. Keith had taken them over pickled in alcohol, which her grandmother had drunk, chillies and all.

"Gran likes her drop of gin now and again," she said without expression. Gran, she implied, could vie with any colonial male.

The other bride was the new Mme Alvarez-Montoya. Although the news of the young doctor's marriage had preceded him, most people had treated it as rumour. Alvarez-Montoya, the flirt, the womaniser, actually getting married. It was impossible. We'd all assumed that he was the sort of person who would avoid getting hitched for as long as possible. Besides, unlike Keith, he hadn't mentioned that he had a girlfriend at home. And on a month's leave, he would barely have had time to get to know a woman, much less court, marry *and* persuade her to come and live with him in this remote part of the world. But as the time came for him to return from his leave, we were assured by M Fontaine himself that the rumour was indeed true.

Being Alvarez-Montoya, there was of course much speculation as to what the woman would be like. She would, naturally, be elegant, mondaine, the crème de la crème of sophisticated womanhood, a glamorous young raven-haired beauty, a Carmen, a clicker of castanets. She had seduced, snared and enmeshed the elusive Alvarez-Montoya with her sexual charms.

She turned out to be none of those things. She was mousy blonde and positively plain, with a long face that made me think of Henry the Eighth's wife Catherine of Aragon. She was also older than Alvarez-Montoya, probably in her mid-thirties. But she was called Carmen. She was shy and spoke neither French nor English, so that her husband had to translate everything that was said. It appeared to be a marriage arranged by his family – she came from his native Catalonia – and probably was. Alvarez-Montoya treated his bride with chivalry and apparent devotion.

To begin with, I befriended Mme Alvarez-Montoya because I felt sorry for her. I knew that it must be very lonely for her at the substation some fifteen miles away when her husband was at work. But we soon became real friends. When I first met her I'd suggested that she join Charles and me at the swimming pool. Alvarez-Montoya arranged for a driver to bring her there most days, and we sat in the sun on the side of the pool. We managed to devise a system of communication based on her school-girl English – she had no French – and my matric Latin.

What endeared me most to my new friend was her love of Charles. She laughed and teased him in her native Catalan. On one occasion when we were alone, she pointed to my tummy, now ripe to bursting, and asked how long.

"Quanto tempo?"

"Any time now," I answered. "A few days, a few weeks, I'm not sure. My first baby was three weeks early." But this didn't satisfy her. There was

160

something more she wanted to know. We tried all the words we knew, but it wasn't until she shyly pointed to her own tummy that I realised what she was trying to say. She was asking me how long it had taken for me to get pregnant. She had been in Elizabetha only a few weeks, but was clearly determined to provide her husband with an heir.

One day we were drinking a Fanta at the clubhouse when we heard the sound of an engine. Cars were a relatively rare phenomenon on the plantation, and besides, this was rather a noisy one. I looked across the valley to see what appeared to be an open-top sports car hurtling along the dirt road.

"Vite, vite," Mme Fontaine called out to her sons, "c'est l'auto de M Meekings." It was indeed Dick's car, and presumably on its maiden voyage. The road ran along one of the hillocks across from a dip near the clubhouse.

"Regardez! Regardez!" Mme Fontaine's son was jumping up and down with excitement.

Dick, beard streaming in the wind, was in the driver's seat, proudly in command of the wheel. Cowering beside him was his unfortunate "boy", who had clearly been given no option but to become his first passenger. He was clinging to his seat. At the back, equally alarmed no doubt, was Dick's dog, Tookey. Just as we were all about to raise a cheer, there was a bang and the car came to a halt. Dick got out, opened up the bonnet, and a belch of smoke rose from the engine.

"Ah, le pauvre M Meekings," Mme Fontaine remarked before resuming her conversation with Mme Delvaux about the best make of pressure cooker.

To me, though, the explosion felt like a real disaster. It was as if Dick's bubble of illusion had blown up. Quite apart from all the time and effort invested, the kit had been expensive, and Dick cared about money.

We were all living in our own bubbles of illusion, and it seemed symbolic.

"You realise that things are hotting up," Jennifer told me on her next visit to the plantation. She, unlike the rest of us, had her feet firmly on the ground. "The CNL are instigating revolts against Adoula's government. They're being funded by the Chinese as well as the Russians."

"Why should the Chinese do that?" At that stage, I knew little about the exiled Conseil National de Libération.

"The Chinese don't just want to change the government. For them, the Congo is ripe for an anti-imperial, anticolonial revolution. According to the stuff I've been picking up, they're training revolutionaries who in turn are training the guerrillas."

"But the United States would never let them get away with it," I said, echoing my husband's philosophy. As long as Adoula's government was in power, David had told me, the West had a vested interest in not allowing anything drastic to happen in the Congo.

"Maybe not, but it's a darn sight too close for comfort. There are a couple of left-wing politicians – Gizenga and Soumialot – who're heirs to Lumumba and are behind it all. They're stirring up the trouble here in the Haut-Congo. My parents are terrified. They keep writing to me and urging me to come home. And frankly, as far as I'm concerned, the sooner the better. I can't stand it here."

I shut my ears. While she was talking, the thought of the Mau Mau uprising in Kenya had flitted briefly through my head. I'd been living in Rhodesia at the time, and what made the whole thing particularly shocking was that, in some cases, it had been the actual servants who had murdered their masters. If they could do that sort of thing there, why couldn't they here? Except, of course, that Nicholas would never, ever hurt us. I knew that.

And besides, I liked it here. And I was so heavily pregnant there was no way I'd be able to leave the plantation now, even if I'd wanted to. I was frantically sewing baby clothes, while Nicholas gazed on in wonder. He was so intrigued by my new machine that eventually he asked if he could have a go. I gave him bits of material to practise on. After that, whenever he had the chance, I would hear the machine clacking away at ever-increasing speeds. It was like a game. Nicholas didn't seem to be worried about what was happening in the Haut-Congo. And surely, I argued, if anyone had their ear to the ground, it was him.

One evening, an old missionary couple from a station further south, came to dinner. They were staying on the plantation overnight on their way home to England, and were due to catch the mail plane in the morning. I hadn't met them before because, as far as I was aware, they'd never visited Elizabetha. In fact, I hadn't even known of their existence. Both were in their seventies, and had lived and worked in the Congo all their married life. What was immediately obvious was that they were quite different from the other missionaries. It was as if they were the equivalent of the vieux colons, while the younger missionaries were nouveaux colons.

Both the missionary and his wife were dedicated; their devotion to God and their need to spread the word was more important to them than anything else. I was shocked when she told me that her vocation took precedence over her children. When they reached the age of four or five, she had taken them back to England to be brought up by relations, before returning once again to her husband.

"It was the climate, the children's health. We didn't feel that it was safe for them out here," she said simply.

"But you missed out on the whole of their childhood," I burst out, unable to contain myself.

163

"We were privileged to be called by the Lord." At that moment, her conviction sounded to me like sanctimony.

On the other hand, it did seem to be a very close marriage. Africa had been their life, and through their shared faith they had grown together so that they were like two ancient trees whose roots and trunks were intertwined. The missionary told me that he had, in his time, translated the whole of the Bible into Lingala. He also knew the language of the drums. There were only two notes, he told us, the male and the female, one high, the other low. The whole of the drum language was based on the sequencing of these two notes. He made it sound like an ancient binary system of sophisticated communication.

"What do they say about the war?" I asked.

The old man shrugged. "It's not good news."

"Are you worried?"

"We managed to weather the storms of 1960, so I don't see why we shouldn't do the same now."

From what I could gather, the mission station had been cut off when the troubles flared up, so the missionary had decided to cycle all the way to Stanleyville, a hundred and fifty miles up-river, to get help. On the surface it sounded like a completely mad venture, but it had been essential. Without intervention the other missionaries on the station would, he implied, have perished.

The roads, as he described them, had been very primitive, in some cases nonexistent. He'd had to ride through swamps, and along dirt tracks through thick jungle. His bicycle had kept getting punctures. It may all have been harebrained, yet the ride had been an adventure. He was the last in a line of missionary adventurers going back to David Livingstone. They wouldn't have been afraid of the rebels wearing feathers and skins. They'd have known the Simbas for the heathens they were.

They'd have talked to them in their own language and dispelled their myths and fancies. It was exactly the sort of story I wanted to hear.

Of course, the old missionary and his wife were an anachronism, but part of me couldn't help admiring their faith in the goodness of humanity. To them, every soul, especially a black one, was worthy of salvation. They wouldn't have wanted to run home like Jennifer at the first sign of trouble. The only reason they were going home was because they were being forced to retire.

The courage of the old missionaries brought everything back into perspective. We were just a backwater. A place you passed on the way to somewhere else. I continued to walk Charles to the swimming pool every day, and to cultivate my potager while I waited for my baby to arrive. We had rows of little beans and lettuces and carrots. It wouldn't be long before we'd be able to entertain like Mme Fontaine and Mme Delvaux. The chickens were less successful, though. They never gave us any eggs, which I assumed was because they were still so scrawny – it didn't occur to me that the eggs were probably being removed and sold back to us. Before we had a chance to find out, however, the venture was sabotaged by the cocks. There were two of them in the little harem. Hearing an unnatural amount of squawking one day, I went out to the pen – only to find a battle in full swing. One of the cocks was almost bald. I told Nicholas to kill them both, and we ate them in a casserole.

Chapter 20

"You can always tell the war drums," Mme Fontaine said at dinner one evening.

There had been talk of the rebels and their leader, Gaston Soumialot. They had got away with a cache of arms and the Congolese troops had been fired on as they drove through the streets of Stanleyville. The conversation was calm, the whole thing dismissed as another bit of local trouble. The reason for the dinner party was because the president at the Brussels head office was visiting the plantation. He had brought his wife with him. The Company would never have allowed them to come if there'd been any serious threat.

For Mme Fontaine, this was her moment of glory. It was like entertaining royalty. All the red carpets had been laid out, all the senior managers and their wives had been summoned. These included, to my surprise, Paul Losonier, M Fontaine's Congolese deputy. It was the first time a black man had been invited to a formal Company dinner party. To Mme Delvaux's chagrin, I had been placed on the right of M le Président himself. Her feathers were ruffled, but she didn't walk out. The president was a worldly man who clearly appreciated young women and automatically flirted with them, even if they were heavily pregnant. He started teasing me about my French.

"I can pronounce grenouilles," I boasted, enjoying his attention.

"Ah, but can you eat them?" he asked, roaring with laughter at the idea of an English person eating frogs.

Mme le Président, a heavy woman, expensively dressed and coiffed, was eyeing her husband from the other side of the table. Our conversation had by this time moved from frogs to telepathy. I was proud of the fact that I could now carry on a conversation, and even crack jokes, in French.

"I bet he doesn't know what I'm thinking now," Mme le Président murmured to John Goodfellow.

The polished table gleamed under the light from the candelabras. The cut glass sparkled. The laughter tinkled. It could have been a sophisticated dinner party anywhere in Europe, except that the servants handing out the gourmet food were black.

"Tell me, doctor," M le Président said, leaning across me and addressing Monge, "how many patients do you have?"

"I don't know exactly," Monge answered. "This is a large plantation."

"And what about the ones in the trees?"

Monge lowered his head and went on eating.

I looked across at Losonier. I couldn't see his face, which was cast in shadow.

"The war drums . . ." Mme Fontaine was saying. "We heard them at Independence."

"How could you tell?" I asked.

"They're low. Frightening. Quite different."

I thought of the language of the drums: high for female, low for male. A language so old and so familiar that it superseded all the different languages that had developed in the aeons since it was first conceived. War had always been the domain of men, I thought, hence the preponderance of male notes. Deep. Elemental. Throbbing. I felt a frisson of fear mixed with excitement. As if the jungle were stirring inside me.

It was the first time anyone had talked openly about what had happened at Independence, though I had heard stories. One was that M Fontaine had been taken out of his house and ordered to cut the grass with a machete. There was, I thought, a wonderfully creative sense of irony in the vision of the proud Belgian cutting his own lawn like a common labourer. John Goodfellow had told us a similar story about his predecessor, who was also an Englishman. He was so large and lazy he'd taken to shouting orders without ever moving himself. At Independence he had been picked up by a couple of workers and frogmarched the five miles along the road they had just built to the next substation in Elizabetha. They had presumably been giving him his comeuppance, but here, too, there'd been no outright violence.

These stories were another indication of how well the whites were known by the Congolese workers. Just like the names they'd given the whites, they had fitted the punishments to the individuals. Because they knew us, I believed, they wouldn't deliberately want any harm to come to us.

The conversation moved on, the way dinner-party conversations do, from war drums to the subject of my nanny. It may have been that Mme Fontaine sensed Mme le Président's exasperation at her husband flirting with younger women as she deftly changed the subject.

"Have you employed a nanny yet?" she asked in a slightly head-girlish sort of way. We had already discussed the possibility of my getting one when we'd met recently at the swimming pool. At the time, I had prevaricated.

"Not yet."

"But do you not think it is getting urgent?"

I didn't like to admit that the reason I hadn't seriously considered getting a nanny was because I didn't think I needed one. Nicholas was only too happy to baby-sit in the evenings or to look after Charles if I went out during the day and, as far as I was concerned, no one could possibly be as loving and trustworthy as he was.

"What about Winifred?" M Fontaine joined in.

"Of course. Winifred. She would be perfect." Madame had a false edge to her voice. She tried to make it sound as if she'd only just thought of the idea.

"Winifred is the daughter of a pastor," M Fontaine explained. "A Church of England pastor," he added triumphantly, as if being somehow affiliated to the English church clinched the question of Winifred's suitability.

Winifred's father, I gathered, had at one time been in charge of the little church on the hill near our house where the lovely singing came from. I imagined he'd called his little daughter after some worthy English missionary's wife. I pictured a good little girl, washed and scrubbed, with a prayer book in her hands.

"She will be perfect for you," Mme Fontaine went on.

"Thank you," I said. I was, in fact, warming to the idea. A pastor's daughter sounded all right.

"I will send a message," M Fontaine said, "and she can come and see you herself."

From Winifred, the conversation switched back to politics. The United Nations had finally left the Congo. Everyone at the table agreed that this was a good thing. Adoula's government had made such a mess that everyone, both in the Congo and outside of it, decided that Moïse Tshombe was their man. So Adoula, the puppet prime minister, had recently been ousted and replaced by Tshombe. Again the general consensus seemed to be that this was a good thing because it would bring Katanga back into the fold.

I was getting more and more confused. It seemed to me that Moïse

Tshombe, however worthy and Christian-educated, had done the dirt on the Congolese government by leading the breakaway Katanga province. This was what had caused all the trouble in the first place. He was a traitor, yet even though he'd behaved so badly, he'd been welcomed back into the fold. But it was not appropriate for me to say anything. This was men's talk. The West had solved the conundrum, we were told, by making Tshombe head of the entire Congo and not just Katanga. Voilà. Two birds with one stone.

"What the country needs," M le Président pronounced with all the pomp and authority of someone in the know, "is a strong leader. That is the only way these blacks will be able to sort themselves out." He helped himself to some more pudding from a bowl held by the "boy" beside him. "It's all a question of evolution. They are not ready for democracy."

No one, I noticed, asked Losonier for his opinion.

The day after the dinner party, Winifred turned up. Instead of going to the back door as was the custom in Elizabetha, she walked up to the front of the house. I could see her from the living room where I was sewing. As I had no idea who she was, I left Nicholas to talk to her. He was cleaning the veranda at the time.

"There's a woman to see you," he said to me, and I could tell from the tone of his voice that he didn't approve.

I went out onto the veranda. It was like being visited by a film star or a model, and for a moment or two I didn't know what to say. Winifred, swathed in bright African prints, was tall and beautiful. It wasn't just this, though, that threw me; it was her poise. She was, without doubt, the most un-nanny-like nanny you could imagine. She had, however, come expecting to work for me, so I invited her into the house and introduced her to Charles.

Since the dinner party, David and I had barely had time to discuss the question of a nanny. Monsieur and Madame had decided that I needed one, and, since what they said generally went, I'd told myself that they were probably right. It would mean that Charles could get used to another woman, and this might soften the blow of a rival brother or sister suddenly making its appearance. I told her she could start the next day.

The first morning was hard work. Winifred not only didn't look the part, she knew absolutely nothing about children. She drifted aimlessly around the house like a bored visitor. When I produced a box of wooden bricks, she toyed with them but seemed more concerned about the state of her fingernails than communicating with Charles. There was none of the female rapport that I had hoped for, either. While I'd accepted that a nanny, in theory, would make life easier, I'd have preferred not to have Winifred. But as the baby was due at any moment, and she had come through M Fontaine, it was awkward.

Pretty soon, Winifred, like Francois in Léopoldville, cottoned on to the fact that I wasn't up to much as a boss. She knew instinctively that I was never going to be able to impose my authority on her. The next day she turned up late and complained of a headache. The day after that she didn't turn up at all. Her excuse was that she wasn't well. But she didn't look remotely ill, and Nicholas informed me that she had gone shopping in Basoko. When I asked her if this was true, she freely admitted it. She made her shopping spree sound like an outing to the nearest provincial town – a Brighton or Eastbourne – not a small, primitive trading post in the back of beyond on the banks of the Congo River. It put Basoko, and indeed the whole social infrastructure of this part of the world, into a new light.

Up till then, I had watched the arrival of the steamer and the daily life in the village behind our house in a detached, almost sentimental way. I'd seen the Congolese people as intrinsically noble as well as primitive. And, as I'd discovered on my visit to the market, they were a world apart from our tiny community of whites. Although my chance encounter with Stella had jolted my sensibilities, it was Winifred who made me aware that black society, even in this part of the world, was just as stratified as ours. Winifred was not only a sophisticated woman of the world, she was clearly a good-time gal. She partied at night and had a lively social life. She was also completely unsuited to the job she'd been employed to do. But though David and I discussed it at length in the evenings, we had no idea what to do about her.

"She's probably Fontaine's mistress," David said.

It was a surprising statement, particularly coming from my husband. But, thinking about it, he was probably right. It was possibly why Mme Fontaine had been so keen to get the girl a proper job. It would give her something to do. On the other hand, it may simply have been a case of an employee asking the general manager to do his sister or cousin a favour. What did become evident from the gossip we picked up, and which was common knowledge, was that Winifred's family had a bad reputation.

Her father had at one time been the Anglican vicar in charge of the little church on the hill near us, but he had lost his position because all his daughters, with the exception of Winifred, had produced illegitimate babies. The church authorities seemed to have decided that if he couldn't keep a check on the morals of his own children, he was unfit to lead a larger flock. The girls sounded to me like vicars' daughters the world over, but I doubted whether in England a father would have been held responsible for the transgressions of his offspring.

As with Francois, I felt awkward and inept. Winifred was infuriating, but I couldn't bring myself to confront her. She was not only a good deal taller and more beautiful than I was, she was more confident. In any other society, I could well have been working for her. It was Nicholas who forced a conclusion. Stupidly, it hadn't occurred to me that he already knew all about Winifred. That she was notorious in the black, as well as the white community.

"She is a bad woman," he told me. Whenever Winifred was about, he became stony-faced and refused to communicate. My loyalties were torn between sisterhood and my friend. As the situation got worse he threw out dark hints.

"What are you going to do about cette femme?" He'd taken to referring to her as "that woman".

Finally, when, after several days – in spite of Winifred's persistently high-handed behaviour and unsuitability for the job – nothing had been resolved, he went on strike. He didn't turn up at his usual time, and when he did eventually make it he worked slowly and sullenly, refusing to look at me. It was completely out of character.

"Nicholas," I wailed, "you can't do this to me. You know the baby is about to be born at any moment."

"What are you going to do about cette femme?" he asked again.

"But I've got to have a nanny to look after Charles."

"I will find someone."

That afternoon, I told David he would have to sack Winifred.

"Why do you always land me with the dirty jobs?" he protested.

"Because she wouldn't take any notice of me," I said.

"Fontaine is going to be furious."

"It's her or Nicholas." That was the clincher. David steeled himself for the job.

When it came to it, Winifred didn't care a hoot. She didn't even bother to say goodbye to me. Looking like a fashion model, she sauntered off down the drive with a month's pay, in lieu of notice, tucked into her bra. I knew that I must have plummeted in the estimation of Mme Fontaine and Mme Delvaux, but with B-day fast approaching, there was nothing I could do about it.

Winifred was replaced by one of Nicholas's relations. She was small and ugly, and she spoke absolutely no French. I had to communicate with her through Nicholas, but she was obliging and perfectly capable of making sure that Charles didn't get into trouble. Nicholas would always be there to supervise, and besides, I didn't plan to be away from home for more than a day or so. The hospital was not very far from our house, and Sister Maria had assured me that Charles could come there as often as I liked. I was a devotee of the child expert Doctor Spock and believed that everything would be all right, provided Charles did not feel in any way usurped. One of the advantages of having the baby on the plantation was that he would be able to continue with his routine and not feel his nose being put out of joint.

By this time, the whole plantation was as excited by the imminent birth as I was. The nuns were all busy praying for us. Alvarez-Montoya had even brought with him a crate of champagne – to celebrate the birth, he claimed. It would be the first white baby born in Elizabetha for years. I felt like royalty. The little hospital had been completely re-decorated in our honour and even given a coat of whitewash on the outside. I'd got everything ready for the new baby. The cot was made up, the clothes neatly stacked and ironed, and I had packed a small suit-case, the way they tell you to in the books, all ready to take with me. In it I had put my baby-doll nightie, a frothy two-piece concoction of white nylon and lace that I had ordered in a moment of extravagance from a Harrods catalogue. It was completely incongruous, I knew, but I wanted to look beautiful and sexy for David after the baby was born.

We'd already decided that, even though David's job was not a particularly demanding one, we would come back after his leave for another term at Elizabetha. It was, we'd told ourselves, a unique experience, one we might never have the chance to live through again. On one of my visits to the convent, I had discussed the possibility of working there after the birth. The sisters had told me they'd be delighted to have some help. I was planning to visit the school with a view to teaching there when the baby was old enough to be left for a few hours. I was also dallying with the idea of a bit of midwifery. I had begun to believe that I could fulfil my dream of contributing to the future of black Africa.

"The minister for sport came through Elizabetha today," David remarked as we relaxed on our veranda, relieved that Winifred was no longer with us.

"Oh? Why?"

"Running away from Stan, apparently. Legging it down to Leo."

"But why should he want to do that?"

"God knows."

I had a surreal picture of a black man, in white running shorts and tennis shoes, sprinting through the jungle waving a tennis racquet.

"Probably belonged to the wrong tribe," David went on. "They're always having feuds."

That was the accepted theory. If anything went wrong, it was always reckoned to be tribal. No one in their heart of hearts really believed that it was us they hated.

PART III

Chapter 21

"Mauvaises nouvelles." Bad news. Four men stood in our doorway: Fontaine, Losonier, Delvaux and a dark-haired, grim-looking man I'd never seen before.

We had only just come indoors from the veranda and were about to start our dinner when we heard the sound of a car driving up to the house.

"Who on earth can that be?" David had remarked. No one ever visited us unexpectedly in the evenings.

There'd been a knock. The door had opened. And there they stood.

I knew from their expressions, even before Fontaine said the fatal words, that something really dreadful had happened. A preview of disasters had flashed through my mind. My parents were dead. There had been a nuclear explosion. Armageddon.

"What is it?"

"Stanleyville has fallen."

For a moment I felt a surge of ridiculous relief. If it was only that . . . Stan was a hundred and fifty miles up-river and . . .

"All the whites have been taken hostage."

Still the full implications didn't sink in.

"You must pack straight away," Fontaine said, addressing me directly. "A boat will take you to Basoko, where you will catch a plane . . ."

"But I can't possibly travel like this." The idea was so ludicrous as to be laughable. Only that morning I had been to the clinic, where Monge had told me that the baby was the right way up with its head well engaged; that I could expect the birth at any moment.

"We have already been to see the doctor," Fontaine persisted.

"But there must be some mistake . . ."

"He will come to visit you himself."

Gradually, the seriousness of the situation was percolating through my consciousness. Stanleyville taken. All the whites kept hostage. They were prisoners. The vision of that dinner we'd had in the restaurant jutting over the river flashed into my mind. I remembered how I'd urged the young Belgian woman I'd met there to stay. To have her baby in the Congo. Would she have to give birth behind enemy lines? It was her first baby . . .

There'd been a radio message from Léopoldville telling the Company that the rebel army had occupied Stan and blocked off all exits. It wouldn't have been hard. All the rebels had to do was take the airport. The roads were no longer usable after Independence. The only other means of escape was down the river, and that could be watched.

The Company had arranged for a small plane to fly to Basoko to evacuate the women and children from Elizabetha. We were to go in two lots; the women with small children first, the rest of the women later.

"You must be down at the beach at dawn," Fontaine was saying, "with no more than forty kilos of luggage." I watched his lips moving. It was as if I were an observer and he was talking to someone else.

"You must carry on as if it were a perfectly normal day. We do not want the workers to know anything about the situation yet in case they try to sabotage your departure. Some of them might be sympathetic to the rebels."

Sympathetic to the rebels. My heart was pounding. The idea was so shocking that I couldn't take it in.

It was a bizarre situation. One part of me was excited by the idea of an adventure, flattered even that Charles and I were to be given priority, while the other part knew that the whole thing was mad. How could I possibly travel over a thousand miles in my condition?

After the men had left, David and I were too shocked to speak.

"We'd better eat," David said.

I had let Nicholas off for the evening, so I went to fetch the dinner he'd left in the oven. It was a casserole. Pink fish with breadcrumbs on top. I put a spoonful on each plate. We both sat there and stared at it.

"You ought to eat something," David said at last.

I tried, but the fish tasted like wood chips.

"I'll go and pack," I said. The initial shock had been replaced by an unnatural calm.

I'd often played the game of what I'd take in case of a fire: books, photos, mementoes; but now, faced with a real choice, I found my mind working clearly and without a trace of sentiment. As the baby would very likely be born somewhere between Elizabetha and Léopoldville, I had to take the carrycot and, depending on the weight allowance, possibly the pram wheels, as well as every nappy we had, all the baby clothes and, of course, food for Charles. I would also take his teddy bear. There wouldn't be room for anything else.

"We'd better send for Nicholas," I said. Some of the essential clothes needed washing.

David called out to the night watchman who was sitting huddled up outside the back door. "If he isn't in his house, go round the beer halls." It wasn't just that we wanted the help, he was part of our family. I needed him. Inside, I felt dead. Everything had been so perfect. Too perfect.

While the night watchman was out, another car drew up outside our house. This time it was the doctor. I had completely forgotten about him. He breezed in, plastered in smiles like a ventriloquist's dummy.

"Pas de problème," he said when I told him I'd been having niggling pre-labour pains, "there is no reason why you should not travel."

Come off it, I wanted to say, who do you think you're bluffing? But somehow, knowing how much this performance was costing the taciturn Monge, normally honest to a fault, I felt bound to go along with his charade.

"I will just give you a petite piqûre," – a little injection – he said, diving for refuge into his bag.

"Why?"

"To make you calm."

"I am calm."

He looked relieved.

"Just tell me what I should do."

"Cry," he said. "It is better for you to cry than to have my injections."

It only occurred to me after he'd left that he hadn't examined me or listened to the baby's heart.

David was right. Nicholas had been in a beer hall. He came into the room swaying. He tried to focus his eyes while David told him what had happened. Then, staring for a moment or two, he turned and, without saying a word, left the room. I heard the tap in the back yard running, and a few moments later he reappeared, shaking drops of water from his head.

"What shall I do?"

Unlike Monge, Nicholas made absolutely no attempt to hide his feelings. He was appalled. While we washed and ironed and packed he kept shaking his head, repeating the same word over and over again: "Mabe . . . mabe . . ." which means "bad" in Lingala. "War bad," he said, as if from a terrible, resigned despair. We were in the same boat. For all of us, it was the end of a dream.

I found myself trying to comfort Nicholas. "You must take everything," I told him, "everything."

He shook his head.

"You can keep the things in your house. Give them to us when we come back."

"What happens if you do not come back?"

"Then you must keep them." Again, he shook his head. "But we will be back." Still he kept shaking his head.

"Look," I said, "here is the sewing machine. It is yours. I give it to you. You can take it back to your house tonight. I shall bring another one from England." Even this didn't cheer him up.

"What will happen to Madame and Charles?" he kept repeating.

"We'll be all right."

"And the new baby?"

"We'll call him Nicholas, after you."

It was after one o'clock when we finally got to bed. The alarm was set for five, but that was unnecessary. Neither David nor I could sleep. We lay huddled in bed clinging on to one another. "Perhaps it'll be born during the night," I said, willing the labour pains. For, at that moment, what I wanted more than anything else in the world was for the baby to be born in Elizabetha, just the way we'd planned. I knew the people here. The villagers would look after us. No one would dream of hurting us. The storm would come and then pass on. Provided we stayed together, everything would be all right.

At five o'clock the alarm went off. Still, the baby had not been born.

It was early, grey-before-dawn, and Charles, sensing that something unusual was happening, leapt up and down in a frenzy of excitement, particularly when I told him that we were going in an aeroplane like the one that flew over the plantation every week bringing the letters. Nicholas

183

was there, too. He had even laid the table for breakfast, but again we could not eat. Everything was packed and ready. I had decided to take my small emergency case with the baby-doll nightie, as well as a larger case and the carrycot. All we had to do was to put my suitcases into the car and leave for the beach.

My last memory of our house in Elizabetha, where we'd lived for a brief five months, is Nicholas watching the car drive away. I can still see his face, his brown eyes urgent with despair, still hear his voice saying "mabe", still feel the tug of guilt that we were leaving him behind.

Just before we got to the beach, I asked David to stop the car so that we could say goodbye in private. As we kissed, I realised for the first time since this whole nightmare had begun that I had no idea what would happen to David and when, if ever, I would see him again. That moment still comes back to me every time I read about an evacuation, or see one on television. Up till then I'd been so calm, so contained, so grown up, but that realisation triggered something.

"I won't leave you." I was clinging to him. "I won't let you go."

"You must."

"I can't." I couldn't stop crying.

"They'll be waiting for us," David said at last.

The sun was only just beginning to come up when we got to the beach. The motorboat, which was normally used to fetch the post, had been pulled up onto the sand where the grey water was lapping. There was an air of excitement. Mme Fontaine and her two sons were already seated in the boat, as were Mme Delvaux and her small daughter. Mme Fontaine was clutching a parcel with bits of silver poking out through the brown paper. Mme Delvaux kept patting her chest. "Ah, mon coeur, mon coeur!" she exclaimed. M Delvaux, who was trying to look important and in control as he organised the stacking of the boat, winced with

184

guilt. The main problem, it seemed, was a huge tin trunk which sat slap in the middle of the boat and took up so much space there was scarcely room for anything else. Charles and I climbed on board and I squeezed myself onto a seat with him on my knees, while more suitcases were piled around us onto the already groaning craft.

The only person missing was young Mme de Malherbe. I scarcely knew her. She never came to the club, and I had recently heard via the grapevine that she was so unhappy she drank a bottle of sherry a day. The reason she was to be on this first planeload was because she was pregnant with her first baby. Then the couple arrived, hurtling down the bumpy hill in a van. M de Malherbe, assistant personnel officer, had a soft blond moustache and fair hair that seemed to have been cut by a lawnmower. I'd been told by Nicholas that, according to the drums, he was "the man who worries too much". With a wife getting through a bottle of sherry a day, it seemed he had much to worry about. He jumped out of his van and started running around, trying to look useful. Madame, very young with dark hair, perched on the stern, alone.

As the boat was pushed off from the shore, M Delvaux leapt on board, neatly avoiding knocking Mme de Malherbe into the water. As M le Personnel, he seemed to have been given the job of looking after us, and was accompanying us over to Basoko. "Ah! Ah!" Mme Delvaux had resumed patting her chest, "Quelle catastrophe!" Superficially, it was a bit like a picnic, an outing. Besides their suitcases, the women had brought baskets and carrier bags stuffed with possessions. The parcel clasped so closely to Mme Fontaine's chest contained, I soon realised, the candelabras. Clearly, this had all happened before; not only at Independence, but presumably during the Second World War. The Belgians were a nation who'd had to get used to being dispossessed.

Ever since I'd kissed David goodbye, I hadn't been able to stop crying.

As the boat, piled with women and luggage, pulled away from the shore, and I saw him standing on the beach looking utterly miserable, I was reminded of Ford Madox Brown's *The Last of England*. In this painting, a young man and woman are caged in a boat full of people and possessions, gazing out over a stormy sea to an uncertain future. We, too, were being ripped from our homes, severed from our loved ones, setting out into unknown waters. Only, I was alone.

Mme Fontaine looked at me disapprovingly. "You mustn't cry," she said tartly, "you will distress the child." But, far from being upset, Charles was revelling in the whole adventure. He sat in the front of the boat bouncing up and down on my knees excitedly and banging against my swollen tummy. With him he had his teddy bear. He didn't care if I cried, and neither did I. Monge was right, the tears were cathartic. I wept not only for David and for myself, caught in a war in which we were unwitting enemies, but also for them, the other side. For my friend Nicholas who had done so much to heal my life and give me back my sense of self. I wept for the chaos that had been imposed on his people.

In spite, or perhaps because, of everything, I had never seen the river looking more beautiful. The delicate lilac faces of the water hyacinth looked so innocent as they drifted past. How could anybody blame them for clogging up the river? They were simply another aspect of nature. It was the same with Elizabetha, which was gradually receding. In spite of the factory, it seemed such a green and pleasant land. A place where people had cleared the jungle to make themselves a habitation. The sun was rising over the plantation and it sparkled on the palm trees. But, as the boat phut-phutted gently past the islands, I felt a tug on my uterus.

We were met at the beach on the other side of the river by the Portuguese trader. He had clearly been forewarned of our arrival. As our plane had not yet arrived, he invited us into his home to wait.

The house was an extension of the shop and we were led through the store, past the rusty tins, the sacks of manioc, the bales of printed cotton, into the kitchen, a large room where his wife was cooking. She had even more children than I'd seen on my last visit. The oldest – a prepubescent girl with little molehill breasts straining the seams of her tight cotton dress – had inherited her mother's elegant good looks. The youngest was still on her back. In between, there were children of varying sizes. It wasn't just the children, or the mother with her baby tied to her back, or the friend crocheting in a chair, but the lack of time pressure and the casual intimacy of everyone in that room that made it feel essentially African.

I rather hoped that we would be asked to stay in the kitchen. But we weren't even introduced to the women. Instead, the trader took us into another room, where we were invited to sit down. In contrast to the kitchen, this room, which was clearly seldom used, had the musty smell of a best parlour. The furniture we sat on was solid, dark teak; the covering cut-moquette. There were china figurines on the mantelpiece and a cheap pietà on the wall. I couldn't imagine the trader and his mistress relaxing here in the evening.

There were eight of us altogether, four women and four children. The trader had offered us coffee, and while we were waiting for it to arrive, I looked at the framed pictures on the piano. There was one of our host in his younger days, still bulky but with a head of thick black hair, and a plump, dark-haired European bride in a frothy white wedding dress. Alongside it was another picture. This time the couple were visibly older, with their own miniature football team going down in a diagonal line. This funny, ugly little man obviously had two lives, two families.

After an interval, his wife brought us coffee on a tray covered with an embroidered cloth that had little beads dangling from its edges. She still didn't talk to us – perhaps she spoke no French – and in that setting and role she seemed strangely diminished. I looked at her face to see if she minded about the shrine to a woman, and a world, so far away and unknown. If she did, she was giving nothing away. She simply put the tray down on the cheap polished table and left. I wondered about their life together; whether she and the trader ever sat in this room; what sort of food they ate; whose culture they would ultimately adopt. I wondered if she loved him.

We were soon told that the plane was on its way, so, leaving a man in charge of the store, the trader drove us out to meet it. I wondered what would happen to him and his family if the rebels turned up at Basoko. The airstrip, where the small mail plane landed every week, consisted of a short tarmac runway in a clearing hacked out of the jungle. As we heard the drone and watched the tiny aeroplane land and then bump its way towards us, I wondered how on earth we were all going to fit inside. Our luggage – and I'm quite sure the others had cheated on their forty kilos – stood in a terrifyingly large pile on the tarmac. There seemed to be some sort of altercation going on between the pilot, M Delvaux and Mme Fontaine about a large cabin trunk. Eventually, having packed as much of it as they could into the hold, we were told to get on board. The suitcases were loaded, and those that couldn't fit were piled into the cabin and squashed into every available nook and cranny. There were only eight seats, including the pilot's. We all sat, squashed together; Charles was on my lap, barely able to move, and Mme de Malherbe sat silently beside me.

As our tiny plane lumbered down the runway, with the seemingly impossible task of getting off the ground and then staying in the air, I found myself strangely calm. In Léopoldville, and even sometimes in Elizabetha, I had been afraid of the unknown. Now that the danger was so palpably real and definable, I wasn't at all apprehensive. The plane strained every muscle, and once in the air it appeared to stay up more by willpower than anything else. I didn't mind being shut up in that little tin box. The war had happened. The boil had burst. And there was nothing I could do except make certain that I, and my children, survived.

Chapter 22

We set off, flying southwards. The plane was making for Alberta, the plantation I'd refused to go to because it looked swampy on the map. I looked down at the mass of tangled green below. It stretched on and away in every direction, endlessly. I wondered how the pilot could possibly know where Alberta was. We were like a tiny, inconsequential bird making for a pinprick in the jungle. We seemed to be following the river – a skein of embroidery silk on a lumpy green counterpane. At times the threads parted to include an island.

Charles started to get restless. He sat fidgeting on my knee and I could feel my tummy contract occasionally. I wondered what would happen if I went into proper labour. My first birth had taken sixteen hours, I reminded myself, so there was nothing serious to worry about. All the same, I glanced at Mme de Malherbe sitting next to me. How would she cope if I gave birth? The plane was so packed there was absolutely nowhere to have the baby anyway. At last, when we had been in the air for several hours, we began to descend. A small rectangular clearing like a long football pitch appeared in the jungle. Then a tarmac strip presented itself. And we hit solid earth.

There was a small group of people waiting beside the runway, a welcoming committee. As well as the managing director of Alberta and his director of personnel, there was a man with a thick moustache who looked like Groucho Marx. He turned out to be the doctor. I had not expected the Company to be so organised. Even here, in the middle of a crisis, protocol was strictly observed. Mme Fontaine, along with her two sons, was ushered into the managing director's car. Mme Delvaux, seated of course in front, with her daughter in the back beside Mme de Malherbe, was to be driven by M le Personnel. Charles and I were to travel with Groucho Marx.

I found myself strangely reluctant to leave my travelling companions. Diverse as we were, a tiny cluster of individuals tossed together by fate, we had begun to form bonds. On the other hand, I was touched that the Company had considered me important enough to send a doctor to meet me. The mystery, though, was that he didn't seem remotely interested in my health. Instead of asking questions, he talked fast and compulsively. I decided that he must be an Italian. His French was so heavily accented that all I could do was say "oui" to the questions he seemed to be asking – or perhaps it was just small talk, as I barely understood a word.

Alberta was flat and felt far more oppressive than Elizabetha. There were no views, just the feeling of being swamped by the palm trees on either side as we drove along a dirt road. And yet, it did have its own character. It had obviously been established far earlier than Elizabetha; most of the houses were old, the sort that might have been there in Conrad's time.

"What happens if I go into labour during the night?" I asked when we arrived at the accountant's house, where Charles and I were to stay. Although I'd been disregarding the periodic tugs in my tummy as there was nothing I could do about them, I did feel that the doctor ought to be taking me more seriously.

"Pas de problème." His mouth split open in a shy smile under the heavy moustache, and he held out his hands. "I have these." Comfortingly large, reassuringly workmanlike, his hands looked as if they could deal with anything from a burst pipe to . . . yes . . . even a delivery. "If you need me, just call out to the night watchman. He will be outside your window. And he will come straight to my house." Or at least, that's what I hoped he'd said.

As with everything else, we were being billeted according to the job and status of our husbands. M le Comptable had a nice house. In fact, when I was shown into our room, I reckoned I had done particularly well. I had been given a double bed. There was even a cot waiting for Charles – though I decided I'd take him to bed with me to make him feel safe. Even better, I could smell the dinner. I knew it was the usual Belgian steak and frites, and salad with lashings of garlic, and I couldn't wait. For, although I'd brought jars of baby food and bananas for Charles to eat en route, I myself hadn't eaten anything for over twenty-four hours.

"Ah!" exclaimed my host, leaping up from the sofa and introducing himself when I went through to the living room, where I noticed that the table was laid for several guests. "You are ready? I will take you to M l'Ingénieur to eat. We have arranged for you to dine with your compatriots, the English engineer and his wife. You would prefer that, yes?"

It was the last thing I wanted. I did not want to be lumped in with my compatriots. On the journey to Alberta, there'd been no question of nationality. The crisis had brought us together. Besides, I wasn't just hungry, I was exhausted, and my plan had been to go to bed straight after dinner. I didn't want to have to make polite conversation with people I had no desire to get to know.

We arrived to find the engineer's household in a state of near-panic. Harry, together with his wife, Janet, and their three children, were to leave the next morning; piles of possessions lay everywhere, waiting to be sorted and packed. I felt sure that they wanted our company even less than I wanted theirs.

Up till then it hadn't occurred to me that we weren't the only ones being evacuated. Alberta was four hundred miles from Stan. But, my hosts explained, the insurrection was spreading quickly, like pustules on a diseased body. The Company had had to hire every light aircraft it could get hold of to shuttle people out of the danger area as fast as possible. It was the first proper news I'd heard, and, for all my unwillingness to be with these people, I was grateful to have the situation explained in my own language.

The meal, however, was another matter. The table was laid with bread, butter, fish paste, and angel cake from a tin. Instead of garlic and frites and a fat juicy steak, I had to make do with a high tea.

Janet, who had only been in Alberta a few months, hated the place. "I'm only too thankful to be going," she said. "It's not right to bring children out here. Have you seen the size of the mosquitoes? The malaria here is so bad that four young children have died during the past year. If I'd known how bad it was, I'd never have agreed to come." I'd been right, after all, about those little grass symbols in the atlas.

When Charles and I arrived back at the accountant's house, there was a party in full swing. All the food, except for a few soggy lettuce leaves and bits of bread, was gone. The pilot of our plane was among the company.

"Once before I carried a pregnant woman, who gave birth on the aeroplane," he was saying. "I swore I'd never do it again."

"What happened?"

There was a sudden silence as they realised I'd come into the room.

I didn't ask what had happened to the woman. I didn't want to know, for I was so overwhelmed with tiredness that I could barely move. We were supposed to be leaving again at the crack of dawn, and all I wanted was to get into bed and sleep.

I walked into our bedroom to find a woman the size of a tank standing at an ironing board. She was dressed in a silk dressing gown, and her hair was in curlers. The iron was plugged precariously into the bedside light socket as she pressed a blue dress. It was Mme l'Électricien from Elizabetha. She must have come out for the holidays, as I'd never met her before. Why, I wanted to ask, was she ironing a dress in the middle of the jungle? And who the hell did she imagine she was curling her hair for? But since she'd never come to the club, I hadn't met her before, and so I had to be polite. She explained that she had arrived with the second planeload of evacuees from Elizabetha. I gathered then that we were to share the double bed. I was too exhausted to argue. I undressed Charles, put him into the cot, and climbed into the bed myself.

As he'd grown more and more tired, Charles had alternated between being fractious and hyperactive, and he now started crying. It didn't help that the light was still on. I could cheerfully have strangled the woman standing there in her spiky rollers, implacably ironing her pale blue dress, while a perfectly good pink one lay discarded on the floor. Then, suddenly, all the lights went off.

"Zut!" exclaimed the voice of Mme l'Électricien. Whether she had managed to fuse the lights with her ironing arrangements, or the generator had simply packed up, I had no idea, but Madame was forced to undress and lumber, somehow, to her side of the bed in the darkness. Both our tummies were so huge that they jutted out over the edge of the bed. Charles yelled for a few minutes, but mercifully his extreme exhaustion sent him to sleep.

As I lay in bed thinking about everything that had happened, and picturing the giant mosquitoes which were, even now perhaps, biting Charles, I heard a cough. I presumed it was the night watchman squatting outside my window, and felt comforted. I was reminded of the doctor's hands. I knew that my fate was, quite literally, in those hands. I could feel the palm trees all around us outside in the inky blackness. I was wrapped in the womb of the jungle and, like my unborn baby, there was nothing I could do but wait.

Chapter 23

The doctor was at the house at five the next morning. This time he drove us to his clinic and gave me a proper internal examination on the table. No longer the jokey Groucho Marx, his thick black eyebrows came together and his forehead wrinkled as he probed me gently with his gloved fingers. Leaving me lying on the table, he went to call his nurse, who was next door. She came in and also examined me, carefully feeling inside. Then she left the room and I heard them talking to each other in low voices. After five minutes or so, he came back.

"Yes," he said, "you may continue your journey."

"Was there any question?"

He didn't answer. Unlike my friend Monge, this doctor didn't even try to lie.

We arrived at the airstrip to find a small fracas going on. Although the rest of the luggage had already been stowed, Mme Fontaine's large cabin trunk was lying on the tarmac.

"I can't carry it," the pilot was saying, "the plane is already overloaded."

"But it has all the children's uniforms," the proud Mme Fontaine pleaded. "My younger son is starting boarding school next term."

The general manager of Alberta was called in to arbitrate. The pilot was adamant. "It's not safe to carry any more. The plane is already overloaded."

"We will try and get it onto another plane, or send it by boat," the manager assured her. But we all knew that that was just so much talk.

What did a box full of school uniforms matter in the middle of a war? As the plane taxied down the runway, leaving the trunk forlorn and abandoned in the middle of the tarmac, I had an absurd vision of a whole lot of children running round the jungle in brand-new blazers and hot, scratchy grey flannels.

I must admit that the pilot's talk the evening before about a woman giving birth on a plane, together with the doctor's obvious doubts about whether it was safe for me to travel, had rattled me a bit. The pre-labour pains had persisted. They hadn't become regular . . . well, not what I called regular . . . but, though I wouldn't have admitted it, they'd been more than a niggle. For even though we'd left the trunk behind, there didn't seem to be that much more room inside the plane. The luggage was still piled in the aisle. Even if I handed Charles over to someone else to hold, I couldn't see how there would be room for the baby to be born. I found myself compulsively doing calculations, trying to work out every conceivable option. Obviously, I couldn't lie down. And there was nowhere I could squat. The ceiling of the plane was too low for me to stand on the seat. I thought of swinging my legs up sideways onto Mme de Malherbe's lap, but there still wouldn't be room for the baby to come out. And if it did, I thought with a mad sort of logic, Mme de Malherbe would be so appalled that she might let it fall. The baby could easily slither under the seat, and then what would we do? As there was no possibility of being able to land the plane in this sort of terrain, all I could do was keep telling myself to hold on until we got to Boende, which was the next leg of the journey.

It wasn't simply a question of holding on, however. As the time passed it became more and more of an endurance test. The journey not only seemed interminable, it was acutely uncomfortable. The plane, which had long since left the river behind, was flying over a green no-man's-

197

land that went on and on as far as the eye could see. At frequent intervals, it fell into air pockets. I'd encountered these before on my first journey to Africa in 1948. Then, as now, it had been the turbulent air over the tropics which had caused them. The plane would fly along for a few minutes and then drop like a stone, leaving our stomachs behind. The Fontaine boys started the ball rolling by vomiting into sickbags which their mother had managed to locate in front of her. Some were then passed backwards, and distributed to the rest of us. Charles went a pale jade and threw up while poor Mme de Malherbe, white and tense, looked the other way. I soon followed. There was a disgusting stench that would have made anyone want to vomit. The sickbags joined the clutter of people and luggage as our little plane battled on.

Charles screamed and kicked in between being sick, so that as well as trying to calculate how I could possibly give birth, I started working out what proportion of the journey we'd done, praying, willing myself to hold on. The engine would rev as the small plane rose in the air and then plummeted again; it seemed a miracle that it stayed up at all. Meanwhile, the tangled jungle stretched before us, providing no possibility of an emergency landing.

We'd been told that the journey would take four hours, but four turned into five, and then nearly six. The only thing in the world I desired was to hit solid earth. Nothing else, not even giving birth, mattered any more. It was a question of endurance. As we bumped on and on, I wondered whether the pilot had misread his compass bearings, now that there was no river to follow. What if he'd lost his way? How might anyone find a clearing in this type of terrain? We couldn't possibly go on flying for ever, as we were bound to run out of fuel. I found myself listening to the sound of the engine, waiting for that final cough, the splutter, as its lifeblood dried up and we hurtled into oblivion.

Instead, after a six-and-a-half-hour trip, we eventually landed on an expanse of tarmac with a small brick building on one side that called itself Boende Airport. We were in the middle of the continent of Africa, right on the equator. As the pilot opened the door, the atmosphere hit us like a blast from a furnace. It was midday, and whether it was because there were no trees around, or because the hot tarmac had roasted the air, the heat was beyond anything I had ever experienced or could have imagined.

We piled out onto the burning asphalt and then, to my astonishment, the pilot began to unload our luggage. Perhaps there was something wrong with the engine, after all? Would we have to wait in this inferno till another plane came to rescue us? We might be stuck here for ever! I looked round at my fellow passengers. Mme Fontaine's hair was wilting. Drops of sweat beaded the down on Mme de Malherbe's upper lip. Even Mme Delvaux was silent. The children's faces looked ashen. We were bedraggled as well as exhausted.

The plane, now empty, taxied down the runway and took off, leaving us with our luggage in the middle of what seemed to be a sea of asphalt. This time there were no welcoming committees. No one to help us. I looked at the small building fifty yards or so away. At that moment, it seemed an unthinkable distance to walk.

"Come," Mme Fontaine said, taking command. Although everyone, including the children, had their own luggage to carry, she ordered the older of her two boys to help me.

There was, in fact, no way I could have carried everything myself – the suitcase, as well as the carrycot in case the baby was born en route. There was also my ridiculous little overnight case containing the baby-doll nightie, which, rather like Charles's teddy, represented some sort of continuum. I put it into the carrycot, and one of the boys took one handle while I lugged my suitcase with my free hand. Charles tried to sit down but the tarmac was so hot he leapt to his feet screaming. He then jumped up and down on the spot, wanting to be carried. One of the Fontaine boys took his arm and dragged him. I can still see the heat rising, the air shimmering over the tarmac, feel the sun burning my flesh. I was convinced I'd never make it.

Somehow, we all managed to stagger over to the brick hut. But as we went inside, I felt my legs turn to water and my head float away. The next thing I knew I was sitting on the floor with someone trying to shove my head between my knees. I was aware of the polished concrete floor and the voices around me. Madame went off to find help and came back with a man. He was, I later found out, a local café owner who'd been seeing his family off to Coquihatville. From Coq they were going to catch the regular plane to Léopoldville.

Clearly, the war was erupting in patches like a bush fire and even here, over five hundred miles from Stanleyville, white people were fleeing. The tiny planes were shuttling backwards and forwards, combing the forest, collecting as many people as they could. We, in the meantime, would have to sit in Boende until our plane returned. It would mean several hours' wait. Up till then I'd felt I was managing. Disregarding the odd pain, the tightening of my uterus, I'd believed I could hold on. I tried to tell myself that at least we were on solid ground. But now I had to face the possibility of giving birth in a hellhole.

"Is there a doctor in Boende?" I heard Mme Fontaine ask the café owner.

"No," he answered, "only some nursing sisters at a convent several miles out of town."

I pictured the cool convent, the nuns in their black habits, and started replanning my life. I'd learned to trust nuns. They would see me through.

The Simbas would never invade a convent. If necessary, I could give birth here, and then fly on. I felt a crazy surge of optimism, just as I had the previous evening when the doctor in Alberta had shown me his huge hands. If the baby was destined to be born here in this obscure little place, delivered by some unknown nuns, then that was its fate. Everything would be all right in the end.

Meanwhile, the café owner, who turned out to be a big-hearted fellow, told Mme Fontaine that he had an air-conditioned room where I could lie down. His accommodation was right beside his café. He would take us there straight away. What's more, he had a friend who also had a car, and he suggested that all the rest of our planeload of women join him.

There are not that many saints in my life, but that man was certainly one of them. When we got to his café, he took me straight into his bedroom and brought me a double whisky. The combination worked miracles. I can still feel the blessedly cool air in that darkened room and taste the whisky.

It wasn't only me that was filled with irrational optimism. After resting I made my way through to the café, where I found a party in full swing. The café owner had invited his friends, whose wives had also just left, to join in, and by the time I emerged from the bedroom, everyone was in a rollicking mood and mildly tipsy. The Elizabetha wives were flirting with the abandoned husbands and the café owner had opened up his cellar.

As I entered the room I was greeted like a star: "Bravo, Madame, bravo!" Charles was playing happily with the older children and I was swept up into the warm fug of friendship. Mme de Malherbe, her dark curls clinging to her face, hugged me.

Everyone was telling their own stories. "I remember . . ."; "During les

201

événements de soixante . . ." The usually standoffish Mme Fontaine, flushed with excitement, looked positively girlish.

"Ah, Madame. Out here life is hard for a woman," one of the men said gallantly.

"But why come to Africa if you cannot cope?" Mme Delvaux, no longer burdened with an overconcerned husband, was a new woman.

"True . . . true . . . it's an adventure . . . Life in Africa is a permanent adventure . . . There is always the unexpected."

The crisis had brought us all together and, at that moment, I loved the Belgians for turning this disaster into a cause for celebration. If we were going to die, at least we'd go out merry, and together.

When it was time to go back to the airport Mme Fontaine tried to pay the café owner, but he waved the money away. "What use is it to me? We are all leaving anyway, God willing. Better that we drink it than the rebels, eh?"

He drove us back to the airport, and I imagined that he and his friends would start the party all over again with the next lot of arrivals. I had no idea what had happened to the second planeload of women and children from Elizabetha. I'd been told that the two Ghanaian wives were on it, and I wondered if they'd been billeted with a white family. All the currents in the jungle were eddying. What about the men left behind in Elizabetha? In the crisis of holding on, I realised that I hadn't even given a thought to my husband.

It was late afternoon by the time our plane came back to fly us on to Léopoldville. The pilot had been flying virtually nonstop for nearly twelve hours. For us, though, it was the last leg of our journey. The alcohol had left us all relaxed, and although I was still aware that I might have the baby at any moment, nothing seemed to matter any more.

This time there were no air pockets. Night fell, and as we flew through

202

the darkness Charles climbed off my knee and crawled to the baby's carrycot, which was perched on top of the luggage at the back of the plane. He climbed into it, and curling himself up, fell asleep. I, too, dozed, and only fully woke up as our little plane started to descend.

Chapter 24

Stepping out of the plane at Léopoldville Airport was one of the most bizarre experiences of my life. For months we had lived in comparative seclusion. Apart from the weekly plane and the fortnightly paquebot, our lives had been punctuated only by the distant drums or the drifts of singing from the little church nearby. We had lived by the gentle rhythms of nature. Now, all my senses were assaulted. I was shocked by the glare of arc lights, the roar of jet engines, the jar of everything going on at the same time. Small planes like ours kept landing and taxiing down the runway.

As we limped across the tarmac, I could hear a voice booming on the loudspeaker: "Réfugiés . . . les réfugiés ici . . . ici les réfugiés . . ."

Up till then I hadn't put a name to our predicament. I had a vision of how we'd appear on a newsreel. A tiny group of jaded refugees joining up with a queue of other refugees, a river of displaced humanity, carrying with them their children and their bundles of possessions. We were a story.

The airport was in turmoil. Everywhere there were American paratroopers with guns. There were also officials with lists. As the queue moved towards the passport office, I could feel our group losing its identity as well as our special closeness. We were being fed back into the so-called civilised world, siphoned off into groups of different nationalities. I glanced up at the departures notice on the wall; the names of the various destinations were written up in large letters. Solidly reassuring names from another life. Brussels . . . Amsterdam . . . Rome . . . London . . .

London? Everything became suddenly clear. London was only a seven- or eight-hour flight away. After our small eight-seater, a jet would be like a moving hotel. Even if I were to give birth on board, it would be luxury after the cramped conditions I'd just endured. I was filled with another surge of wild optimism. Having managed to hang on so far, I felt omnipotent. I could fly to London where we would be automatically picked up, rescued and looked after. At last I was in charge of my own destiny.

Somewhere in the mêlée inside the airport I caught a glimpse of Mme Fontaine. Gone was the flushed girl, she was back to her old self again, gathering up her children and organising her luggage. She was still clutching the brown parcel with its silver bits sticking out. The school uniforms may not have made it, but the candelabras had. "Vite . . . vite . . ." she was saying to the children as she hurried them towards the departure lounge, and then, catching sight of me: "Ah, Madame, au revoir." She handed the parcel over to her son in order to shake hands formally. "Le petit Charles," she said, giving him a peck, "et le bébé. Bonne chance . . . à bientôt." And then she and her children were swept away into the crowd, whirled off to another world, and to safety. Again, I felt a tug at parting.

I glanced at my watch. The plane I'd decided on would leave in the next half hour. "We'll go to London," I said when it came to my turn, but the woman with the clipboard didn't seem to be listening. "Ah, Mme Cecil." I was, of course, instantly identifiable. "The doctor is waiting for you."

"The doctor?"

"Come with me. This way, please."

How could I not have thought of that? The Company were bound to send someone to the airport to meet me.

It was Dr Stoppie who was waiting by the customs barrier. He'd been Dr Kokou's second in command. I remembered him well from our days in Léopoldville, though his hair was mussed and needed cutting, and his teeth were in a terrible state. I wondered why he had let himself go so badly.

"Madame," he said, clicking his heels formally, "ça va?"

"I'm fine," I said. "Pas de problème . . . mais . . . "

"You come with me, oui."

"Well . . . non," I said. "I thought I would catch the next plane for London . . ."

"First I must make an examination."

"But what about the plane?"

"There will be other planes."

"I need to get back to England."

"I will take you to the clinic and if everything is in order you may leave."

He must have known things weren't in order. I have since learned that there were radio messages flying from the offices of Elizabetha to Alberta, from Alberta to Léopoldville, and from Léopoldville to the Company's head office in London. I was hot news. Had I or my baby perished, they'd have had a scandal on their hands. It was no use protesting or trying to tell Dr Stoppie that I was all right; I was Company property. Putting Charles and me into his car, he drove us back to Léopoldville. All I could do was hope that the journey into town and the examination would not take too long. I consoled myself with the certainty that this was just another little blip in my journey. Soon I would be on my way to London.

We drove from the airport to town, just as I had a lifetime before. I remembered David's throwaway remark about bandits. Now, the roads were full of tanks and armoured cars. We'd been so naïve in those days.

I was impatient to leave, to get the examination over with, get back to the airport, and take off for Europe. It was one thing giving birth in Elizabetha, where I knew everyone and everything, but to be stuck in Léopoldville was quite another.

We got back to the clinic and, as before, I climbed onto the table so that Dr Stoppie could examine me.

"Eh, bien," he said, peeling off his gloves and washing his hands.

"When can I go?"

"Je regrette, Madame," Dr Stoppie was always scrupulously formal and polite, "there is no possibility of travelling. You are already well dilated."

I suppose I'd known it all along. Something in me had been disregarding the pains, passing them off as unimportant. But at that moment it felt like malign fate. I'd managed to hang on for so long. And just as England, with all the safety and security that it represented, seemed a mere skip away, I was thwarted. Everyone else would be allowed to go on with their journeys except me.

I was also very worried about Charles. The journey had been hard for me, but at least I'd known what was happening; for him, it must have been utterly bewildering. He had been torn from his home, thrown about in a tiny, overcrowded tin box which had made him horribly sick, then dumped in a strange, noisy airport, and now he was about to experience the shock of a new brother or sister. At least if we'd made it to England he'd have had someone to look after him. Here, there were no such certainties. I found myself wishing that I was back with my little group of women: Mme Delvaux, who'd become unexpectedly feisty, Mme de Malherbe, so young and carrying such a well of private sorrow, and Mme Fontaine, our head girl. She would have seen me through. She would have made certain that we were all right.

But, even as Dr Stoppie drove me to the club, where, he told me, I could wash and have a meal and a rest, I started to hatch a new plan. Léopold-ville, and above all the club, was the last place on earth I'd have chosen to be, but at least I'd made it this far. And if I hadn't spotted those airport notice boards, I wouldn't even have thought of getting to England.

The club hadn't changed. The same smell of beer and Gitanes. The same group of men, their backs turned, clustered round the bar. I didn't know any of them and they were far too occupied to be interested in me or my predicament. They were talking about the war, that much I knew. I sensed that they were only concerned with the possible loss of their goods and chattels, or something equally trivial and meaningless. Up till then, my driving concern, my only concern, had been for Charles and the unborn baby. Now, seeing those men drinking beer and worry-ing about themselves, I was flooded with anger. They didn't care a damn about the other Company employees stuck up there in the Haut-Congo. At that moment I had absolutely no idea what was happening to my husband.

We were shown into an airy room with a couple of beds and a cot. I looked round it with an expert eye. It was large enough, and clean. It would do fine.

"We're going to stay here now," I told Charles. "You lie down and have a little sleep." But he wasn't having any of that. His nap on the plane had given him a boost of energy. He was ready for anything. There was nothing for it but to take him back into the bar area. I ordered a juice for him and a medicinal double whisky for myself.

"I need a nanny," I said to the barman. "Do you know of anyone?"

"I have a sister," he replied, as if this were the most natural request in the world.

"I need her straight away. Could she come now?"

"I will see."

At that moment, I spotted Bob Jones in the bar. Although I'd heartily disliked him when we'd lived in Léopoldville, he was, at least, a familiar face.

"Bob," I shouted, greeting him like a long-lost friend.

"Just popped in for a quick beer and an update on the situation," he said.

"How's Janette?"

"Fine. You must come round . . . that is if . . . when . . . Jannie would love to see you . . . and of course if there's anything we can do . . ." I felt a glow of gratitude. I was no longer a stranger in a strange city. Somebody cared. At that moment I loved Bob. How could I ever have thought ill of him?

We were too late for dinner, but the kitchen staff produced some sandwiches. We were just finishing when the barman turned up with his sister. She was an intelligent-looking young woman who spoke good French. I took her into my bedroom and showed her the layout.

"I would like you to look after my child while I give birth," I told her, introducing her to Charles.

I had worked it all out. I'd have the baby in the guesthouse so that Charles would be able to stay with me as long as possible. During the actual birth, she could take him outside. Afterwards, he could come back and climb into bed with me, and he and I and the new baby would all snuggle up together.

Ever since Dr Stoppie had told me I was already dilated, I'd allowed myself to feel the pains. They weren't very strong yet, but I'd started timing them and they were coming at exact fifteen-minute intervals. Throughout my pregnancy I'd had complete faith that the labour would be straightforward and easy. Now, with this responsible-seeming Congolese woman – she was certainly no Winifred – to share my fate, I was even

209

more confident. I felt an absurd pride in myself that I had managed to organise the whole thing so efficiently. That's what a colonial upbringing did for you, I told myself. I'd been taught to cope in emergencies.

My plan may have seemed flawless to me, but Dr Stoppie had other ideas. Since leaving us, he had arranged for me to go into hospital. He soon arrived back to tell me so.

"But I am going to have my baby here."

He shook his head. "Pas possible."

"But I can't leave Charles."

"You will have to find someone for him to stay with. A friend."

"I can't. Not at this time of night."

"It is an emergency."

I felt distraught. How could I possibly abandon my precious child? I pleaded with the doctor but he simply shook his head: "Pas possible . . ." It was always that. Not possible.

This was worse than anything that had so far happened on my journey. There was no way I could leave Charles with a strange nanny. Dr Stoppie pointed to the telephone in the bar. He would wait, he said, while I rang my friends. Frantically, I combed my mind trying to think of people I'd got to know in the six months before we'd left for Elizabetha. Nothing, no one. In any case, how could I ring people up at eleven o'clock at night? Everyone would be in bed. And then I thought of Janette Jones. Bob had only just left the club, so she'd probably still be awake. Having had young children herself, she was bound to know how to deal with a distressed two-year-old.

It was Bob who answered the phone. "Hang on a second," he said, "I'll go and ask Jannie." He left me hanging on for some time, and when he eventually got back to the phone he sounded awkward. "Sorry, love, she's not feeling too well . . . it's her time of the month . . ."

Her time of the month. I'd always thought of her as milk and water. Now she was mere water.

I started going through the directory. Erica was deeply sympathetic, but she was leaving for South Africa first thing in the morning. The women from the Embassy had already been evacuated. Another friend was sorry . . . under any other circumstances . . . but at the moment . . . and so it went on. I began to feel more and more desperate and demoralised. Every rejection felt like a wound. It was far easier to bear physical pain than the thought of my child having to go somewhere he wasn't wanted. As a last effort I tried my Hungarian friend, Pitou Mezzi. I didn't know her at all well, and I found myself already making excuses: her son Zolica was the same age as Charles, and together they would be an impossible handful.

Pitou said yes without hesitation. What's more, she knew where she could borrow another cot. No, it didn't matter in the least that it was nearly midnight, she'd wake her neighbours up. Her husband Zoltan would be round straight away to fetch Charles.

While we were waiting for him to arrive, Mme Alvarez-Montoya turned up at the club. She was among the second load of evacuees from Elizabetha – the rest had managed to get onto planes for Europe. We may not have had a language in common, but that was irrelevant. At that moment the Spanish bride Carmen felt like a true soul mate.

"Prego," she enquired, "Charles?" She pointed to herself, making gestures. It took a few seconds, but eventually I realised what she was trying to say. Somehow, instinctively, she had realised what was happening and was offering to look after him.

"But you're going back to Spain . . . Espagna . . ."

"Non . . . non . . . I stay with Charles." She'd begun to learn English as well as French, and spoke both with an accent.

211

I was so touched, so grateful, that had she arrived a few minutes earlier I might well have taken her up on her offer. What I didn't realise – though at that stage it was too early to tell – was that she herself was pregnant.

Pitou was true to her word, and within minutes Zoltan arrived to collect Charles. It was horrible having to let go of him. Although Charles was almost two, he was a late talker. I'd done my best to explain what was happening, but I had no idea how much he'd understood. He looked baffled as Zoltan scooped him up and carried him off to his car. I felt lost. As if I was in the middle of a storm. I had no idea what was going to happen to any of us. The pains were coming more frequently now, and Dr Stoppie was waiting impatiently.

As soon as we arrived at the hospital I was taken into the delivery room. It was large and bare, and the floor and the walls were lined with white tiles. In the middle there was half a bed with stirrups dangling down from the ceiling. It looked more like a torture chamber than a place for giving birth. I climbed onto the bed and put my feet into the stirrups – there was nowhere else for them to go.

The nurse took my blood pressure, Dr Stoppie examined me again, and then listened to the baby's heart. I could tell from his face that there was something wrong.

"There is foetal distress," I heard him murmur to the nurse in French.

I would like to think that the subsequent events were due to my efforts. My mind over my matter. That, knowing the baby's heart was in trouble, I somehow programmed my labour accordingly. It was probably more true, though, that by this stage my body was entirely exhausted. Whatever the reason, the contractions simply petered away and I lay on the half-bed in the middle of that bleak room, legs hoisted up above my head, waiting. I lay for what seemed an eternity in that undignified position, aware of every cranny being exposed in the cruel light directed towards my vagina. Absolutely nothing happened. I knew I was being a nuisance. Dr Stoppie looked utterly worn out. From time to time he would glance at his watch. Eventually, he gave up.

"Call me when labour resumes," he said to the midwife, and left.

I was then allowed to climb off the delivery table and lie down on a proper bed in a nearby room.

I can't remember sleeping, though I must have dozed off at some stage, and when, by about five o'clock, nothing more had happened, I got up and asked the nurse whether I could go home.

She shrugged: "Pourquoi pas?" Why not, indeed? So, picking up my little suitcase, I set off for the club. I knew my geography. It wasn't far away.

The sun was just coming up as I waddled back along the familiar streets. Because of the time of day, the air was deliciously cool. The small sandy gardens seemed to burgeon in the early-morning light. It was an aspect of Léopoldville that I had never before experienced. In spite of everything, I felt light and airy. I didn't think about David or Charles. I didn't even think about my baby's distressed heart. Once again, I was in charge. Once again, I felt absolutely certain that we'd win.

The club was in turmoil. Small planes had been arriving throughout the night, and the dining room was packed with refugees on their way back to where they originally came from. I didn't recognise anyone. When I felt I decently could, I rang Pitou and told her what had happened.

"As soon as I have finished here I will come round to the club," she said.

Charles arrived in high spirits. He took very little notice of me. He had found a friend, so why should he worry about his mother? I felt both hurt and silly that I'd made a mountain out of a molehill the evening

213

before. The two little boys went straight to the sandpit and started to throw sand at one another.

"It has been like this since early morning," Pitou told me. "I got up to find that they had both got out of their cots and were raiding the fridge. The whole kitchen was a mess." It was typical. Charles was able to reach practically anything. "I put them back into their cots," she went on, "and I tied a dressing-gown cord to each of their ankles to keep them there." It sounded a bit dangerous to me, but I had to trust Pitou.

"He won't be with you for long," I assured her. I had made up my mind that the baby's foetal distress was due to bumping around in an aeroplane for two days, possibly aided by the double whiskys. Because I was "well dilated", my labour was bound to start off again at any moment, and when it did, I was sure the birth would be fast and uncomplicated.

Although the boys appeared to be playing together quite happily, when it was time for Pitou to leave, Charles refused to budge.

"It's all right, darling," I reassured him, "as soon as the baby's born Mummy will be back." His face puckered up. And then he started to scream. I picked him up, but he kicked and screamed even louder. The more I tried to explain, the more he screamed. Then his little friend Zolica started to cry in sympathy. The club was packed with people and suitcases coming and going, with the staff frantically trying to arrange accommodation or transport. People looked at us, appalled. It was as if Charles had created a focus for all their pent-up rage and anxiety.

He kicked and screamed all the way to Pitou's car, and then, as Pitou tried to prise him away, he clung to me as if his life depended on it. She opened the door, and as I tried to put him in he clung to me even harder, screaming and refusing to let go. Pitou had to go over to the other side and yank Charles's legs while I prised him off me and slammed the door on him. Pitou put her son in the front and locked all the doors. It was awful. Charles had done nothing wrong, and yet he was being treated like a lunatic or a criminal by his own mother. It must have felt to him like the final betrayal.

Frantically, I blew kisses at Charles and waved at him through the car window as Pitou drove away. His face was screwed up and grubby with tears. He refused to look at me.

"I think it's better if we don't come and see you again until after the baby's born," Pitou said later on the telephone. She wasn't angry or upset, she was simply being practical. I tried to remind myself that, compared to the scenes that had taken place in Hungary in 1956, this was surely nothing to Pitou.

"I think you're right."

It felt like an admission of failure. This was exactly what I'd spent the whole of my pregnancy trying to avoid. I was a piece of flotsam flung hither and thither by gigantic waves of fate.

Chapter 25

In spite of the war, Léopoldville was still in radio contact with Elizabetha and, by the time dawn broke with me waddling back to the club,
the news of our safe arrival had already reached the plantation. In England the Company had alerted my mother-in-law – my own parents were
still in Iran – telling her to wait on standby in case we did manage to
make it back home. But, even if the European tom-toms were working
reasonably efficiently, and the evacuation of women and children from
the Company's scattered plantations was going ahead without any apparent hitches, head office had little idea of what was actually happening in the jungle. As the pustules of rebellion grew and spread, the Company had to rely on the general managers of each individual plantation
to decide if, and when, to evacuate its staff.

After seeing us off that Wednesday morning, David had gone back to
his office to find Fontaine in a hideous dilemma. He was extremely reluctant to pull the white managers out of Elizabetha because that would
mean closing down the factory, with the consequent financial losses to
the Company. On the other hand, if anything were to happen to the whites,
he would be held responsible. To be fair to him, at this stage the world
press was not taking the capture of Stanleyville all that seriously. The
Congolese government maintained that the army – the Armée Nationale
Congolaise – had everything in hand, and it would only be a matter of
days before Stan would be recaptured and order restored.

With the first batch of women and children safely off the plantation,

Fontaine had called a meeting of all the men in charge of the various divisions of the workforce. From them he learned that there were, indeed, rebel sympathisers among the huge numbers of local Congolese employed by the Company. It meant that if the white managers wanted to leave, they could only do so with the permission of all their employees, otherwise their departure would be sabotaged. So, having weighed up all the facts, and in consultation with head office, Fontaine had decided not to go ahead with a full evacuation. Most of the workers were keen to keep the factory running and to carry on working. He did, however, tell all the managers to go home at lunchtime and to pack a bag in case they had to make a quick getaway. They were allowed an overnight case and no more.

Poor Nicholas. Having been upset by my departure, he was even more distressed to find David packing as well. David tried to reassure him that this was only in case of an emergency. But when three white men he'd never seen before turned up at the house after lunch, all his worst fears seemed to be confirmed. They turned out to be missionaries from three of the stations – Yelemba, Lungungu and Bakondo – who, on hearing news of the fall of Stanleyville, had all decided, quite independently, to up and leave their stations and make for Elizabetha. They had left the other missionaries, along with their wives and children, down at the beach, waiting for instructions. My friend Jennifer, who had kept me informed of political affairs and had been determined to get out of the Congo long before her baby was due to be born, was among them.

David took the three missionaries to see Fontaine. By then, the second contingent of women had just left Elizabetha and were crossing the river to Basoko to catch a plane to Alberta. Fontaine therefore suggested that the missionaries take a boat over to Basoko and try and persuade the pilot to make another trip.

Late that afternoon, David had a visit from Dick Meekings.

"That insurance you were talking about," Dick said, feigning nonchalance, "I've been considering it and I think perhaps after all . . ." Of course, David was forced to decline the application.

By evening, the missionaries had come back. The pilot had been flying all day and refused to contemplate another trip. Fontaine, who seemed to feel responsible for the well-being of all the Europeans round about, tried to arrange for the missionaries to go back across the river to Basoko immediately, where a lorry would pick them up the next morning. But Jennifer put her foot down. So they spent the night in Elizabetha and set off for Basoko on the Thursday morning. As it happened, the decision not to spend the night in Basoko was unfortunate as they just missed a lift.

That morning, the Italian ambassador had flown in. A number of Italians living at Yangambi, a small trading post halfway between Stanleyville and Basoko, had sent an SOS informing their embassy they were marooned. The Italian ambassador himself had set off to rescue his compatriots. Had there been anyone in Basoko needing to get out, his plane would naturally have taken them back to Léopoldville. As things turned out, it returned empty. The missionaries arrived just in time to see the plane take off. They had no alternative but to climb into the lorry, as originally arranged, and make their way to Mokaria.

The Italian ambassador had spent the whole day trying to arrange for a boat to take him up-river to where his compatriots were still marooned. It was an act of cavalier bravery. There were only two boats at the little trading station. The captain of one of them, the *Tshopo*, refused to carry him because it was, by this time, too dangerous. Eventually, however, the intrepid ambassador managed to persuade the drunken driver of the other boat to set off up-river into enemy territory.

Meanwhile, back in Elizabetha, any hopes Fontaine may have had that the capture of Stanleyville was not serious and that the Congolese army would re-establish order were smashed. On Friday, Elizabetha woke to news of an invasion. Overnight, members of the routed army fleeing from the Simbas had arrived on the plantation. Several people in Elizabetha had been woken by disorderly soldiers banging on their doors and demanding money. Most had little to give. M Verbruggen had, so his story went, stood up to them.

"They broke down my door and I found myself with a rifle at my head. The soldier, although I can't call him a soldier – he was a coward, and I told him so – he said that he had already shot two Belgians in Stanleyville and that if I did not hand over my money he would do the same to me. 'Okay,' I said, 'then I will be the third!' So they left me alone. Went away with nothing."

Fortunately, both David and John Goodfellow's houses, which were well away from the road, were left alone. The fleeing soldiers did, however, pick on Dick Meekings. During the night he'd been woken by his dog Tookey frantically barking. According to him, he'd opened his door, only to be knocked down with a rifle butt. But Tookey went for them.

"Before I knew what was happening, I found myself lying on the ground with a gun barrel at my stomach and Tookey there beside me. Dead."

Poor Tookey. And poor Dick. Unlike the brave Verbruggen, he'd not had the courage to stand up to his attackers. When they demanded that he pay up or be shot he waved at the fridge, where his savings were stored in wads in the freezer compartment. The soldiers had had to wait while the fridge defrosted in order to extract Dick's frozen assets.

These crimes were committed by government troops who, in theory, were supposed to be protecting the expatriates. Three of the Company's lorries and one pick-up were stolen – one of the lorries turned up later in a ditch. As the fleeing army straggled through the plantation, a group of them were spotted in a van marked BMS Yakusu. This was the mission station closest to Stanleyville, and had been our first stop on our journey down-river. It was where we had taken tea with the Scottish missionary and his wife and baby daughter. No one had any idea what had happened to them. As usual, though, it was the Congolese who took the worst of the flack. The demoralised soldiers had wandered into a camp of workers and started shouting at them and ordering them about. Having thrown their weight around, the soldiers picked out a handful of victims, beat them up and dragged them into the forest. None of the workers seemed to know whether they were dead or alive. Extraordinarily, despite all this, work continued in the factory.

On Friday evening, the contingent of Italians – nineteen of them – arrived at Elizabetha after being rescued by their ambassador. Despite the insurrection all around them, they had managed to get down-river without any trouble. A young Scandinavian also turned up out of the blue. He had made his way down-river with two Alsatian dogs. "I swear to you," he said, "all the villagers that I met wanted to eat me."

Later that evening, the fugitives all left Elizabetha. This time, the Italians had had to pay the captain of the *Tshopo* a lot of extra money to take them to Lisala, about one hundred and fifty miles down-river through Simba territory. With them, they took the Scandinavian and his dogs. After that, apart from the Catholic nuns who insisted on staying put, the only white people left at Elizabetha were the managers. They decided to group together for safety and sleep in a cluster of three houses, including the tiny guesthouse.

Although no one, neither army nor fugitives, came through the plantation on the Saturday, the men decided to keep the same sleeping arrangements that night. In the morning, David and John Goodfellow decided to return to their own homes and, as it was Sunday, David went back to bed for a lie-in. He was woken at nine by Nicholas, who told him that a drunken soldier had just come to the door. Nicholas had managed to persuade the soldier that there was no one at home, but he had seen him weave his way along the road towards John's house. Feeling that he could not possibly leave John to fend for himself, David immediately leapt out of bed and into his car. He arrived at John's house to find the soldier making himself at home and swigging a bottle of beer.

"The bugger came and asked for one," John muttered under his breath. He had decided to try and keep the man happy until he either went away of his own accord, or help arrived. Having finished his drink, the man opened the breech of his gun to make sure it was loaded, and demanded some money.

"I don't keep money in the house," John parried. "This is the account-ant. If you don't believe me, ask him. He'll tell you. All the money is at the office." The soldier, who appeared to accept this explanation, asked for meat and whisky instead and got given both.

Although the soldier was drunk and volatile, he was not aggressive. In fact, he was positively servile in the presence of the white men. But when one of the works councillors, alerted by John's houseboy, turned up at the scene, he changed dramatically and started shouting and waving his rifle about, threatening to shoot everyone in sight. In this situation, it was David, the gentle, scholarly chartered accountant, who kept his cool and took the initiative. He persuaded the soldier to go with him to see Fontaine – it had been decided the evening before that, in an emergency, the Company would give fleeing soldiers money to placate them.

The soldier tamely complied, and drove with David and John to Fontaine's house. On being given a thousand Congolese francs – a few pounds at the black market rate of exchange – he did a little dance of thanks. When he left the house, however, he was immediately picked up by Losonier and a couple of councillors who had, by this time, been alerted. They relieved him of his gun and marched him off to the Elizabetha jail to sober up.

All this I heard later – I hadn't even known that there was a jail on the plantation. I was immensely proud of David's calm, his courage. As an English boy brought up in a sheltered environment, nothing would have prepared him for that situation. He'd not only shown loyalty in going to the rescue of John, he'd also had the guts to keep his head when dealing with real danger. Yet I was disturbed by the story. The ingratiating dance of thanks made the soldier seem like a submissive performing bear.

This drunken soldier appeared to be the last straggler. Yet when the managers went to work that Monday morning, everyone acknowledged the situation was serious. Elizabetha was the only source of vehicles and petrol in that part of the world, so the Simbas were bound to arrive sooner or later. As far as the whites were concerned, the soldier they'd captured may have been prepared to be bought off, but none of them could have deluded themselves that the real enemy, the Simbas, were anything like that. The rebels had already proved that they were neither submissive nor malleable. And they were gaining converts all the time. It wasn't surprising that the workers, fed up with a government that had delivered nothing but broken promises since Independence, were turning to the rebels in increasing numbers. The big question was how many of the workers were loyal, and whether they would let the white managers escape.

Chapter 26

Stuck in the club in Léopoldville, I had no idea that all this was going on. The Company still had radio contact with Elizabetha, but whenever I asked for news I was invariably told that everything was under control and there was nothing to worry about. In the meantime, I was forced to sit around waiting for my labour to start again. Not that I did much sitting. I ran. I jumped. I squatted. I went for long walks. I did everything in my power to get it going again. Refugees continued to pour through the club. They brought with them their own stories, which merely made things worse.

The first news I got of David was from Jennifer. There was a wait before she could catch her plane back to England so she, along with her fellow missionaries, had turned up at the club.

"He's fine," she assured me airily. And then went on to tell me of her escape.

It was dramatic enough. Having crossed and recrossed the river, and then missed the Italian ambassador's plane, the band of missionaries had eventually made it to Mokaria where they'd had to hire a boat and make their way to Lisala. From there they'd managed to hitch a lift on one of the Company planes. It wasn't fair, I knew, but as Jennifer was telling me her story, I found myself growing more and more angry and resentful. All the missionaries, including the men, had got out on Company transport, while my husband, a Company employee, was still up in the plantation.

As my baby sat in my womb, refusing to budge, the hysteria all around continued to mount. The war was escalating so rapidly that the rebels, so rumour went, were already in Brazzaville, poised to cross the river to Léopoldville. I felt numb with impotence and anger. All I wanted, all I prayed for now, was to be able to drop the baby like a cat, pick my children up, and run. I was becoming increasingly desperate. On one of my walks I passed Dr Stoppie's house. He had so many children that a regatta of white sheets flew on the rows of washing lines. In my desperation, I considered knocking on the door and asking Mrs Stoppie if she had any hints for getting labour going again.

It was at this point, not knowing what was happening to David, or how Charles was feeling, or indeed when, if ever, I'd go into labour again, that I spotted Mr Van Royan. He'd been playing tennis, and his face was bright red. Without looking around, he had flopped his sweaty body into a deck chair on the veranda of the club and ordered a beer.

"Mr Van Royan!"

He turned, broke into a smile, and began to get up. "Why did you not tell us you were in Léopoldville?"

"I thought you must have heard –"

"My wife will be so pleased."

"She's here?"

"Of course."

I hadn't thought of Mrs Van Royan when I was phoning round to find someone to look after Charles. It was partly because I'd only thought of the young mothers, but also because I'd assumed she was still in the Netherlands with her daughter Clara.

"I will go home now," Mr Van Royan said, downing his beer in one gulp. "I will tell Cora and she will be back."

Twenty minutes later, Mrs Van Royan was indeed back. Just the sight of her fat little Volkswagen coming up the drive of the guesthouse made me feel better.

"Why did you not telephone? I could have looked after Charles. Clara is at school, so we have an empty room."

Mrs Van Royan, my substitute mother, my guardian angel. Not only warm and understanding, she also knew about life. She assured me that the baby would be all right and that I would go back into labour.

"The body has a wisdom of its own," she soothed.

After catching up on news, she left, making me promise to call her if I went into labour during the night.

"I'll be here tomorrow morning," she said. "And I will bring you anything you need."

As it happened, there were a couple of things I did need. I had asked an English nurse, one of the refugees still dribbling through Léopoldville, if there was anything I could do about my predicament.

"It's because you're overanxious and exhausted," she'd said with reassuring practicality. "Your body hasn't got the strength. Relax, take plenty of rest; then take some glucose to raise your blood sugar; and as soon as you feel your first contraction, take a good dose of castor oil. That should keep you going." Her instructions had sounded comfortingly like a recipe for making a cake. Although Mrs Van Royan was sceptical about the efficacy of the nurse's prescription, she said she'd try to find the ingredients.

One of the things that had been troubling me was Charles's birthday the next day. He'd be two years old and I wouldn't be there. Although Pitou rang me regularly with news and told me how well Charles and Zolica were getting on, I was missing him horribly. I didn't feel I could tell her about his birthday because I knew she had enough on her plate. On the other hand, although Charles wouldn't be aware of the day's significance, I hated the idea of him not being able to celebrate. Mrs Van Royan did her best. She would go and visit Charles, she said, and she would take him a cake from Le Petit Pâtisserie.

"In the evening we will celebrate ourselves. We will have a dinner party. Play bridge. I will invite Thoby. Just like the old days, not so? You could stay the night. Sleep in the flat."

Miraculously, Mrs Van Royan had managed to get the glucose and castor oil from a chemist. When she arrived to fetch me the next evening, I swallowed a large dose of glucose. As I would be spending the night in her flat, I packed the castor oil in the emergency suitcase – which I took with me, just in case.

Chapter 27

David had arrived at the office on Monday morning only to be told of Fontaine's decision to try to get all the white men out of Elizabetha. Over the weekend there had been urgent discussions among them as to what they were going to do. Some of them, including Dick, were finding the strain intolerable and were frankly terrified. The possibility of evacuating all but two or three of the managers and leaving an administrative skeleton to run the operations had been discussed, but by Monday even this solution had been rejected. The situation was too dangerous. Although none of the Simbas had actually appeared on the plantation yet, they were reported to be in Basoko. They could arrive at any moment.

"We will have to consult the workers first," Fontaine told the men. He had toyed with the idea of sneaking out at dead of night, but had come to the conclusion that trying to leave the plantation without calling a meeting of the entire workforce and getting their permission would be too risky. If the white men were caught they'd be massacred. Everything depended on the cooperation of the black workers.

The traditional African way of solving issues was by calling a meeting. When the white men got to the factory, all the people who worked on the land, as well as in the factories, were there. The managers climbed the factory steps so that they had some sort of platform. In front of them were two thousand men who held their fate in their hands.

The head of the works council spoke first. He explained that the white men had decided that, because of the situation, they needed to leave.

"Why should they?" one man shouted. "What will happen to us?"

The tension grew. There were more angry voices. And then M Fontaine held up his hand and called for silence. Whether it was because of the power of the white man, or the tradition of the indaba, it worked.

Fontaine had prepared his speech, which was carefully translated into Lingala by the head of the works council. He spoke for nearly an hour, and during that time he argued that, in spite of the danger, the white managers had stayed this long to keep the factory going. The Company, he assured them, had the best interests of the workers at heart. If and when the Simbas arrived, they would not necessarily want to harm the workers. But they would certainly kill the white managers. If this were to happen, the Company would be very angry. It would mean not just a temporary closure of the factories, but a permanent one.

"Provided you let us leave unharmed," he argued, "the Company will continue to pay you. Then, when the troubles are over, which will probably be in a week or two, the managers will come back. After that, the work on the plantation and in the factory can resume. It will be like it was before."

It was a risky speech. A bit like picking his way through a forest of pangas – which some of the workers who used them to cut down the fruit were still holding. But Fontaine was an astute manager. He'd been through Independence and was counting on the belief that employment was more important to the men than their loyalty to a group of untried revolutionaries.

A vote was taken by a show of hands. Those in favour of letting the white men go were asked to raise their hands. There was a surge of arms and the works councillors went round counting the votes. "Thank God," John Goodfellow murmured. But when it came to those against, there was another surge of arms – almost identical in number, it seemed, to the first.

The dozen whites stood mute with shock. Although Fontaine had known there'd been a swing of sympathy to the Simbas, he'd had no idea of the extent of it. What's more, by this stage there was absolutely nothing he, or anyone else, could do. They waited, tense with anxiety, for the second lot of arms to be counted. They knew that at that moment they were utterly at the mercy of the workers.

The councillors consulted among themselves. After achingly long deliberations, the head of the council told Fontaine that the majority had voted in favour of allowing the white men to leave the plantation. Fontaine's gamble had come off. The managers were free to go.

There was, however, still the question of where they would go, and what mode of transport they would use. The enemy were, by this time, in Basoko, so there was no possibility of flying out. The one baleinière left in Basoko had been commandeered by the Simbas, while the *Tshopo*, which had taken the Italians to Lisala, had been requisitioned by the Congolese army. They still claimed they could stem the tide. The only possibility was to climb on board one of the tankers which were used to take palm oil down-river.

And so David left the plantation – as he had arrived – by boat. Apart from pyjamas, a change of clothing and a toothbrush, he'd had to leave everything behind: the silver tea set we'd been given as a wedding present by his grandmother, all our books and family photographs, and a dozen bottles of best malt whisky that had arrived with the most recent hamper. He, too, had told Nicholas to take whatever he wanted – and hoped he wouldn't drink all the whisky in one go.

Alvarez-Montoya had decided that, if he took nothing else, his case of vintage champagne counted as essential luggage, and Dick Meekings, having lost Tookey, refused to be parted from his stuffed crocodile. After the terrible strain of the last few days, there was an atmosphere of hysterical jubilation as the men boarded their improbable vessel and set off down the river. The crate of champagne proved useful as a seat, and some of the others must have wished they'd had the same idea. In the general mêlée, Alvarez-Montoya had trodden on the jaw of the stuffed crocodile, breaking a tooth. Dick accused him of doing it on purpose, but Alvarez-Montoya warned that if he wasn't careful, his crocodile would be tipped overboard to join its brothers and sisters in the river. In the middle of this fracas Dick spotted a canoe in the distance behind them.

"Here, there's someone following us." Everyone assumed he was joking, but when they heard the distant sound of a motor, there could be no mistaking it.

At first they tried to pretend that it was of no significance, but as the boat started to catch up on them, it became obvious that they were being chased. They could see that there was only one person on board, but that was not particularly comforting. Everyone assumed that the occupant was almost certainly armed with a gun.

"Perhaps it's a disaffected worker," someone ventured. What no one said – though the same thought was going through everyone's mind – was that it was a Simba, determined not to let the white men escape.

They asked the driver of the tanker to go faster, but the bulky vessel was not built for speed and everyone realised that it could only be a matter of time before the boat caught up with them. There followed a terrifying chase while the smaller boat relentlessly came nearer. No one dared look backwards.

As it drew closer the men heard a voice shouting at them in French. "Alors . . . messieurs . . . Arrêtez-vous!"

Although the face in the boat was white, it wasn't until he came close that they recognised the Portuguese trader. Everyone assumed that he had fled along with the others.

The general relief was tinged with unease as the boat drew up alongside the tanker. Everyone presumed he had chased them in order to hitch a lift – but instead he took a package from his boat. It was a bundle of letters. "If you could post these," he said, "they're to my family in Europe. I don't know when I'll next get the chance to write." Then he turned around and motored up-river, back to his other family, and straight into enemy territory.

Alvarez-Montoya opened one of the bottles of champagne.

"To the success of our trip . . . "

The bottle didn't last long. Its empty carcass was tossed into the river.

"Now we drink to the baby." Alvarez-Montoya opened another bottle, then a third in case it was twins, and so it went on until there was a trail of champagne bottles joining the water hyacinths in the wake of the boat.

"To all fathers," Alvarez-Montoya toasted, giving Dick a wink.

Dick spluttered, "I'll have you up for libel. I've only been here six months."

Even though the journey was to take the rest of that day and the whole of the night, it was, by all accounts, a jolly lark. And nobody mentioned the three black managers who had been left behind.

Chapter 28

"Seven hearts," I called.

It was just over a year since I'd first been in the Van Royans' apartment. Its rugs, its rough linen curtains, everything was imbued with a patina of shared contentment. It all felt like yesterday. Conversely, in spite of the fact that it was only just over a week since the four men had arrived at our house in Elizabetha and overturned our lives with the words "Mauvaises nouvelles", it felt at that moment like another existence; something that had happened to someone else in a dream. Perhaps it was this sense of permanence within impermanence that filled me with hope. In spite of the war going on out there, I felt safe in that flat. I clung to the belief that the Company would get David out.

I looked at the Van Royans. They had come through the Japanese concentration camps and survived. Mr Van Royan had recovered from his bad turn. His blood pressure was back to normal and he was his old, assured self. Mrs Van Royan, as always, was calm and strong. Even Thoby seemed more grown up, less cocky and sure of himself.

That evening the cards were with me and, in spite of the fact that Thoby was not nearly as good a bridge player as David, we couldn't go wrong. I didn't need fine eyes because all my finesses worked. It was grand slam time. I was in a particularly reckless mood and my overbidding came off.

We played on and on, reluctantly going to bed at about one thirty in the morning. I dropped into bed and fell immediately into a deep sleep. At four thirty I was woken by a serious pain. There was no doubting it this time. The baby was, thank God, once more on its way. I swallowed the half-bottle of castor oil to help things along, and then I woke Mrs Van Royan.

As we drove through Léopoldville in the darkness, everywhere was silent. Eerie, even. There was a breathless quality in the air as if the enemy were poised and about to pounce. Now that I was back in the business of giving birth, I could seriously contemplate the situation and try and work out contingency plans. I knew the enemy were on the other side of the black, oily river. I knew that there was no time to lose. And I knew that I would have to give birth as fast as possible in order to get my children out safely. My little suitcase was with me. It, too, had made it all the way from Elizabetha.

We rang the bell of the hospital and were shown into a small reception room; the woman who had let us in said she would call someone. Mrs Van Royan took out her knitting while I prepared to give birth. Every time I felt a contraction coming, I would go into a squatting position to try and speed things up.

"Are you sure you should be doing that?" Mrs Van Royan asked.

I wasn't sure, but I couldn't risk the labour stopping again.

We waited. I squatted with each contraction. Mrs Van Royan knitted. And still nobody came.

Suddenly Mrs Van Royan suspended her needles in midair to look at her watch. "My God," she exclaimed, "the last one was only two minutes ago."

Even I had not realised how fast my labour was moving. I could see that Mrs Van Royan was beginning to panic. She hurried out of the room in search of a nurse. A few minutes later, she came back even more agitated.

"I cannot find anyone."

233

It didn't take us long to realise that all the sisters were saying their early-morning prayers. Once again Mrs Van Royan hurried out, this time in search of the chapel. She returned with a nun.

I never did ask what happened, but as soon as the nun appeared everything started moving. Mrs Van Royan was sent off in her Volkswagen to fetch the doctor, while the nurse, who was clearly flustered, took me into the delivery room. The same white box, lined with tiles, the same hard, truncated bed in the centre, the same stirrups dangling from the ceiling like hangmen's nooses.

"Non, non," the nurse cried out in agitation as I leapt onto the table, "vos pieds ne sont pas antiseptique."

The impulse to give birth had become so overwhelming that the cleanliness of my feet was the last thing I cared about. I was aware of a surreal element to the whole scene. All I wanted to do was to get on with the whole business. The nurse, on the other hand, seemed determined to try and prevent it. Having climbed off the table – I'd never really fancied it anyway, particularly with no one at the other end to catch the baby – I looked round for a suitable spot. A room, a field, anywhere at all would have been better than this hard white box. The only solution I could see was to squat down, lean against the wall, and have the baby right there. Even then, I worried that its poor little head might come in for a crack.

Squatting down and leaning against the wall seemed to trouble the nurse as much as my leaping onto the delivery table with dirty feet.

"You cannot wear a dress."

"Then what can I wear?" It seemed to me that the hospital must surely have a gown. Besides, the question of what I should wear was, by this time, as academic as the state of my feet. All the nurse needed to do was pull off my knickers.

"You have no nightgown?"

I directed her to the suitcase, which I'd left in the waiting room.

She came back a moment later.

"This is all I can find." In her hand she carried the piece of white ny-lon froth. I put it on. There was a large satin bow in front, from which flowed a fully gathered skirt. It was cute enough, but even if you included the frill round the hem, it barely covered my navel, and under the cir-cumstances the knickers were redundant. It would have been far less indecent wearing nothing at all.

I still worry about the sensibilities of that poor nun as I sprinted round and round that large, bare delivery room in my baby-doll nightie. Eve-ry now and again, when the urge became too great, I would squat down in a corner, panting like a dog.

"Non, non," the nurse would cry anxiously, "pas là."

"Where, then?" The castor oil had begun to churn up my stomach. Moments later, sitting on the lavatory, I was convinced I was going to give birth in the pan.

The nurse's anxiety increased – I later discovered that the nuns were not supposed to deliver babies without a doctor being present.

In the meantime, while I was running round the delivery room, being thwarted at every turn, the Company was busy evacuating all the women and children. Pitou and little Zolica were being flown out of Léopoldville. And unbeknown to me, Charles was once again motherless and aban-doned. I never did discover what happened to him during that time, though he was probably left at the club with somebody in charge of him. Fortunately, I was oblivious of it all at the time, and when at last Mrs Van Royan returned with Dr Stoppie, I was allowed to climb back onto the table – I still hadn't washed my feet – and get on with the urgent business at hand.

The reason that the doctor had no car was because his driver had used it to take his wife and children to Matadi. The town was about two hundred miles down-river, and from there they were planning to catch a boat back to Europe. Dr Stoppie looked pasty-faced and moth-eaten as he washed his hands and prepared himself to deliver my baby. He had brought with him a newspaper, which was lying on the trolley with all the instruments. Even in full labour I couldn't miss the words "Haut-Congo" in bold print on the front page.

"Un vrai massacre," Dr Stoppie murmured to the nurse who was glancing at the headline.

Part of me felt outraged. How dare they talk of massacres when I was giving birth? They must have known that my husband was in the thick of it. It was as if they thought they were dealing exclusively with the bottom end of me and that the top didn't exist. I wanted to tell Dr Stoppie smartly to get on with the job at hand. At some stage, it occurred to me that in England I'd have been offered painkillers or gas and air. Here, I didn't even have the luxury of suffering. All I dared hope, at that moment, was that the doctor would concentrate so that he'd be able to catch the baby when it came out.

I needn't have worried. My daughter slithered into the competent hands of the midwife, and, apart from having a bit of mucus sucked out of her windpipe, she was absolutely perfect. I was flooded with euphoria. I wanted to climb straight off the table, dance round that dreadful white room and drink champagne. I had pulled it off.

The doctor, ever polite, clicked his heels and, addressing the top half of me, said, "Congratulations, Madame," then left.

I had been transferred onto a trolley and was lying there, sore but triumphant, when the nurse who had helped deliver the baby came back. She put her arm on my tummy and leant on it, hard. It was agony, like going through a birth all over again. I delivered another large chunk of what I presumed to be afterbirth.

Looking back on it all, I am aware of how extraordinarily lucky I was. I had prayed that Jessica – we'd already decided on the name if the baby was a girl – would be born on the night we were told we had to leave the plantation. Thank God she wasn't. The journey to Léopoldville would have been far, far more gruelling with a baby. It was even luckier that she wasn't born in the plane, where her chances of survival, I later discovered, would have been very low. But luckiest of all was the fact that she'd not been born en route: without the attention of a qualified midwife, the bit left inside me would have gone bad and I would have died in the jungle of puerperal fever.

With plenty to be thankful for, I was still lying on the trolley when a priest arrived.

"I'm going to be sick," I said as he started to read a prayer.

Displaying an alacrity born, presumably, of long practice, he whipped out a kidney bowl. He was just in time. I could only hope he hadn't taken my remark personally.

As Jessica was the only white baby in the hospital there was no need to label her. We were wheeled into a private room with its own bathroom, where she was washed and oiled and we were left alone to get to know one another. I picked her up and started to suckle her. Then we both went to sleep.

I was woken a few hours later by a knock on the door. To my utter amazement, David and Charles walked in. I could scarcely believe it. Both my men were alive, well and, most important of all, with me. There were hugs and kisses. And tears poured down our faces.

Having admired the baby, David couldn't wait to tell me about his adventures. "It was incredibly hairy . . ." he started.

A hairbrush came hurtling across the room. It was aimed at the baby. It missed, but Charles already had a pretty good eye, even at the age of two years and one day.

Chapter 29

David heard about his daughter's birth at a place called Bumba, the one-time capital of the Congo, four hundred miles down-river from Elizabetha. They'd been travelling on the tanker for a day and a night, and on arrival at Bumba Fontaine made contact with the Company in Léopoldville via the local radio. He then handed David a note written in immaculate copperplate: "Cher Monsieur Cecil, Leo m'annonce que Madame a accouché ce matin d'une fille, tout le monde se porte bien. Sincères félicitations. J Molderez." Dear Mr Cecil, Leo tells me that Madame gave birth this morning to a daughter. Everyone is well. Sincere congratulations. It was dated 11.8.64, though in fact Jessica was born on the twelfth. But after all the worries and anxieties, Fontaine can be forgiven for being a day out.

Although there was quite a crowd of people waiting to be flown out of Bumba, and although they included women and children, it was generally agreed that David should travel on the next available plane. So it was that at about four thirty that afternoon, as if to order and with perfect timing, there was a knock on the door and he walked in with Charles. It seemed nothing short of a miracle.

As soon as I could, I left the hospital and went back to the club. The atmosphere was completely different from when I'd left only a few days before. It was as if an avalanche had swept away the white female population. Practically the only European woman left in Léopoldville, it seemed, was Mrs Van Royan. Most of the managers from Elizabetha were there.

Like schoolboys, they were tumbling over one another with their tales of valour and derringdo. Everyone told me how brave David had been.

"He was very worried about you and the baby," Monge said at one stage, as if he had read my mind. For David was still on such a high after his experiences that it didn't appear he'd given us a thought.

The shared adventure had bonded the men just as it had us women. Back at the plantation, they'd been individuals in their own right. Added to this, their position within the Company hierarchy had given them an identity. But now, the urban setting somehow diminished them. I was particularly aware of this when I saw Dick Meekings dressed up and ready to fly back to England – the Company by this time was repatriating all but a bare skeleton of managers. He was dressed in a rather cheap Terylene suit and had shaved off his beard. No longer the aspiring Somerset Maugham character manfully building his own car in the middle of the jungle, he looked what he was: a provincial English lad with few social graces.

Apart from Fontaine, who went into the office every day, frantically trying to work out what was going to happen to Elizabetha, most of the men had nothing to do but sit around in the club every day. Even Monge was idle.

"I tell you," he admitted one evening over a beer, "I have never had to take a medical decision like that before in my life, and I hope I never do again. I was not only afraid for the baby, I was afraid for you. If you had given birth on that aeroplane . . ."

"I was never going to die," I assured him.

All the same, I could see that, from his point of view, it had been an impossible choice. He'd had to weigh up the risks of the journey against those of a possible invasion. I could only thank God he'd opted for the evacuation.

There was another difficult decision that Monge had had to make, and he was remarkably frank about it. It turned out that he did indeed have two black children: two daughters, by two different common-law wives. He'd had to decide what to do about that. In the event, he and his wives had opted to get his daughters out. For had the Simbas invaded, two children with white blood in them wouldn't have stood a chance. So, although the mothers had to be left behind, Monge had put his two little daughters onto one of the planes leaving Basoko. From there, they would fly to Léopoldville and on to Brussels, where they would be taken to a Catholic boarding school.

"But you're Spanish," I said.

"They will be better off in Belgium," he answered. "And I will be able to visit them whenever I am in Europe."

But how did the mothers feel? I wanted to ask. Monge was a conscientious man, he wouldn't have taken the decision lightly. I imagined that he envisaged bringing his daughters out to Elizabetha for an annual school holiday, at least. Working abroad always involved heartbreaking separations.

There was, however, one decision that was almost impossible to justify, and that was leaving the three black managers behind in Elizabetha – "to find their own way through the jungle" was how it was put. Fontaine usually made all the decisions, so he was presumably responsible for this one.

"We were crammed together on the tanker," David said, "there was no more room."

"There was enough room for a stuffed crocodile and a crate of champagne."

"I felt very bad about it."

How did Fontaine justify it? Perhaps he told himself that they were the skeleton he was leaving behind. Perhaps he really did believe that the Congolese army would gain control. Yet he must have known that if the Simbas were to invade Elizabetha, the managers, particularly the Ghanaians, would have had virtually no chance of survival.

There were also the Catholic nuns, of course. Unlike the missionaries, they'd opted to stay with the people who needed them, despite the Company's responsibility to evacuate them. They were women of God. And the Congolese people, they believed, respected religion.

Another odd decision was to fly me and the children out of Léopoldville without my husband when Jessica was under a week old. The Company, or more probably Fontaine, decided that David should stay in Léopoldville in case management were able to get back to Elizabetha. In those days, jobs took precedence over families. David didn't think to question it, and neither did I. Yearning for my mother to look after me, I opted to fly to Iran instead of back to England. It was a crazy decision.

When we took off, however, and I looked down from the safety of the airliner at the immensity of Africa, I felt a surge of relief. I was getting out. I was going back to civilisation. From now on, everything was going to be all right. Or at least that's what I assumed. We were VIPs, to be indulged and cosseted. Jessica was the youngest passenger ever to fly on that airliner – the previous incumbent in the logbook was the pope. I was sloughing off all responsibility.

We had to change planes en route to Iran, so were scheduled to spend the night in Rome. Yet by the time we'd reached our hotel and I'd fed Jessica and tried to calm Charles, it was already morning. We were due to fly out early, but the American airline we were booked on refused to carry us because I had no visa. Even though I explained that my father would be meeting me at Teheran Airport with the visa, they refused to budge, shoving the rulebook at me. Having missed a night's sleep, I had to wait the whole day in a filthy terminal, in apparent limbo. Charles was so frantic that he lay kicking and screaming on the floor, his face caked with dirt. I was too exhausted to do anything about it. And Jessica couldn't stop crying, probably because I was running out of milk. There was no one, it seemed, to help us. Eventually, that evening, an Italian airline agreed to carry us. They pointed out that I had a return ticket and was allowed into Iran for forty-eight hours without a visa. The stewardess coaxed the distraught Charles to eat a meal, and he went to sleep. Trying to feed my starving baby, I hung onto the thought of home. The nightmare, I told myself, would soon be over.

There was no one at Teheran to meet us. I waited and waited. Even though I'd been assured by both airlines that my parents had been told about the altered arrangements, they didn't turn up. By now it was three thirty in the morning. I had missed a second night's sleep and could barely stand up, much less think. I can still see the expanse of deserted terminal as all the other passengers dribbled away. Not only did I have no visa, I had no money. I was alone, by myself, with two small children, in a strange Middle Eastern country.

And then, while I was trying unsuccessfully to make a reverse charge call to my parents on the telephone, a French oil magnate I'd spoken to on the plane turned up. Though he had a company car waiting outside, he'd been concerned when he didn't see us emerge, so he'd come back into the terminal to see what had happened. He was a small, round man, and reminded me a bit of Agatha Christie's Hercule Poirot. I knew that one should never trust strangers, particularly men who offered to take you back to their hotel in the middle of the night, yet I no longer cared. He could have had whatever wicked way he wanted at that stage – not that I could have been a very alluring proposition. He drove us back to Teheran, booked us into a hotel room, and telephoned my parents. They had slept through the previous telephone calls, but woke to this one. They gave his driver directions, and at last I was being driven home. The exhaustion I felt was beyond anything I'd so far endured. I was like a watch, wound up so tight that it could no longer tick. I was too tired even to want to die.

A few weeks later, David was finally evacuated and joined me in Teheran. We went on a brief holiday, but I was still exhausted – too exhausted to appreciate the fabled sights of Iran. Shortly afterwards, we all went back to England and to rented accommodation in London and picked up our lives. David, who was still working for the Company, was moved to a different department. Only, of course, it wasn't that easy.

"By the way," he said over dinner one evening, "you were right about Wilkinson and Mme Bossart."

"What about them?"

"They were having an affair."

"How do you know?"

"Bossart confided in me. He asked me what he should do, because he'd discovered that his wife was sleeping with his boss." David was chortling at the ludicrousness of it.

"How could anyone be afraid of sad, puffed-up little Wilkinson?" I snapped.

"Bossart was afraid of losing his job."

"Oh, for God's sake. If he's not man enough to confront his boss . . ." I was losing my sense of humour. It was all so petty, so inconsequential; a tiny scribble in an already overfull, chaotic notebook.

Other things made me flare with anger. Like the story of the man whose wife had lent me her radio in Léopoldville: it had been stolen just before we'd left for Elizabetha, and he'd been heard boasting at the club bar that, although he'd got David to repay the full value of it in sterling,

244

he'd claimed on his insurance as well. David had been a sucker. I'd been a sucker. We'd been minnows in a pond full of piranhas. One lot got fat on the others.

And there were so many lies. Quite by chance, we were told by someone that one of the missionaries, it may even have been Jennifer, had boasted that she'd stayed in Léopoldville to help me out while I had my baby. I wouldn't have minded this so much had the nightmare of that evening, when everyone rejected my child, not stayed with me.

We kept up with the news, of course. There was triumph when Stanleyville was retaken. The Belgian paratroopers had flown in, but, with the news of their coming, the rebels holding the town had forced all their hostages into the central square and opened fire. It had been one big, almighty shootout; the stuff of the *OK Corral*. Bang, bang, you're dead – until only the good guys were left. But in the films you know who the goodies are, and you don't care about the rest. And the hero, of course, always survives. Who were the goodies and the baddies here, though? In this game, the most ruthless always won and the weakest went to the wall.

Mrs Van Royan told me later about the planes she'd met carrying rescued hostages from Stanleyville. "They were full of orphans," she said, "children whose parents had thrown themselves in front of their offspring when the rebels opened fire in the square." In the face of such selflessness, the brutality of the rebels was beyond contemplation.

With the liberation of Stanleyville, news of the full horror of what had been happening in the Haut-Congo, the land of Lumumba, began to seep out. Looting, burning, people chopped to pieces. Nothing was sacrosanct. Even nuns, the newspapers reported, had been raped. Inhumanity which equalled that of King Léopold's time. Was this to be the story of Africa? And was one the inevitable consequence of the other?

On leaving the Congo, I entered my own heart of darkness, what might now be called post-traumatic stress disorder. I had become allergic to civilisation. I found the noise, the pace, the greed intolerable. When I went into a supermarket I got the shakes; when I went down into the London underground I couldn't breathe properly. Corridors would close in on me; my limbs would become paralysed with fear. I felt like an ant. For it seemed to me that we humans, black and white, were no more than fodder for the corporations to get rich on.

And I, too, was guilty. I was haunted by what may have happened to the young Belgian woman I'd talked to over dinner beside the Congo River in Stanleyville. Unless she'd managed to get out earlier, she'd have given birth behind enemy lines. And it was I who'd urged her to stay. In some obscure way, I felt I should have been there, not her.

One ordinary November evening, with the dead leaves sticking to the wet pavements, or lying windblown in corner heaps in our suburban garden, David came home from work to a flat draped, as ever, in nappies and sodden baby clothes.

"By the way," he remarked over supper, "they've got news from Elizabetha."

"What?" My heart seemed to contract. My first thought was for Nicholas. I'd thought about him a lot since we'd left. In fact, I couldn't stop thinking about him. Apart from the way he had helped me through and made me a whole person again, we had left him with a poisoned chalice. Our European possessions would have been worse than useless to him. A positive hindrance, in fact. He'd have been considered a European stooge. And once they'd found him out, the Simbas would have shown no mercy.

"Miraculously, Losonier made it all the way to Leo . . ." David was saying. Losonier, a Congolese, would have spoken Lingala.

"And the Ghanaians?"

"God knows. I imagine they were picked up by the rebels. All they said was that twelve people were lined up against the store at Elizabetha and shot . . ."

Twelve people. They'd have been all the foreigners, rounded up by the Simbas. Those who weren't there already would have made their way to the plantation somehow in dugout canoes, just as they had before David left. The Portuguese trader . . . the nuns . . . the vieux colons . . . the nouveaux colons . . . I could see them all: the people who had stayed behind through a sense of duty or necessity, or because nobody had bothered about them. But it was those black Ghanaian managers that really haunted me. How could the gentle, Dickens-loving Edward possibly have made it through the jungle with no local language? His family was probably proud of him when he was chosen by the Company as a manager. He'd got onto the first rung and was making his way up the white man's ladder.

The Company had helped all sorts of other people to escape: foreigners, missionaries, anyone who wanted to get out of danger – provided they were white. And so I'd survived. But I'd learned that it was impossible to come out with your hands clean.

Afterword

At Jessica's wedding, thirty years after our escape from the Congo, I made a speech. She was working for the BBC at the time, and I told her fellow producers and presenters that, ever since her birth in the Congo, she'd wanted to be in the eye of a political storm. From a very young age she'd listened to the radio and quizzed disconcerted grown-ups about their opinions on current events. It was almost as if the massive upheavals that were taking place while she was in my womb had somehow percolated through the placenta; as if she'd been born to be a citizen of the world. The reason I was making the speech was because David had died ten years previously of a heart attack; it was Charles, therefore, who'd given his sister away.

In spite of the traumas Charles had had to undergo before and during Jessica's birth, he had turned out to be a kind and sanguine man with a wonderful sense of fun. He was running his own company producing interactive computer games – something his father would have been unable to conceive of.

David himself never lost his taste for Africa. During our stay in Nigeria a year later, the Company made sure I got out in time. The baby arrived early, though, only just missing the Biafran War. We went on to have a fourth baby, who was born in our bed in London. This would undoubtedly have disappointed Nicholas – as far as he was concerned, I was supposed to be the mother of sons. All three girls turned out to be strong and independent, holding down good jobs.

What I am overwhelmingly aware of now is how young David and I were when we set off for the Congo on our grand adventure. Both of us were in our twenties. Although we were open to new experiences, we also thought we knew it all.

When I'd first got to Léopoldville I'd naïvely used the metaphor of an emerging butterfly to describe the newly independent country. Certainly, the Congo was rich in resources – but this was the reason for outsiders wanting to get their hands on it: first King Léopold, and after Independence, the international powers, including the company David worked for.

I couldn't help wondering what David, who always defended the status quo, would have made of a BBC report in October 2000. In it, the correspondent exposed the Belgian government's masterminding of the secession of mineral-rich Katanga. The Belgians had used Moïse Tshombe to do their dirty work for them. And when the United Nations arrived on the scene, they were thwarted by "Belgian civilian personnel". It became clear to me, years later, that the newly independent government had never had a hope of getting off the ground.

Working hand in glove with the Belgians, the Americans had plotted the "definitive elimination" of Patrice Lumumba. His murder reads like the script of a horror film. The CIA initially planned to poison him with toothpaste, brought over by a CIA agent calling himself "Joe from Paris". The local CIA chief in Léopoldville had, however, been so appalled at the plan that he had thrown the toothpaste tube into the Congo River. From then on, Lumumba was hunted like an animal. He tried to escape upriver to Stanleyville but was captured by his erstwhile ally, Colonel Mobutu. When he appealed to local UN troops for help, they "refused on direct orders from headquarters in New York". He was flown back to Léopoldville, where he was physically brutalised and then chained to the back of a truck and dragged bleeding along the ground. After that, he was taken to Mobutu's villa and beaten up in front of television cameras.

As a final torture, Lumumba was despatched to Elizabethville in Katanga, and into the hands of his archenemy, the pro-Belgian stooge Moïse Tshombe. Having been abused once again, he was eventually executed by a firing squad assembled and commanded by a Belgian. The missionary-educated Tshombe was present throughout. Lumumba's body was first buried in a shallow grave, then exhumed and dissolved in acid and burned to destroy the remains. One of the two men who carried this out, a Belgian, told the BBC: "We were there for two days. We did things an animal wouldn't do. That's why we were drunk. Stone drunk."

The real facts of history would not only explain the "stagnant calm" we experienced in Léopoldville, it would explain why Katanga was reunited with the rest of the Congo and Moïse Tshombe put in charge of the whole country. He didn't last long, though. He was ousted by Mobutu, whose brutal reign continued for the next thirty-five years. It would be comforting to argue that if Lumumba had survived things might have been different. But even then, it is difficult to see how the Congo, with all its wealth, could possibly have resisted power politics and the avarice of the rest of the world.

"The downfall of the Congo was due to our greed," I recently remarked to Gerard Pambu, a Congolese who'd had to flee to England when he crossed swords with Mobutu. We were sitting in his office in a bleak part of London in the bleakest of winter weather. "Corporate greed. International greed."

"And African greed – Congolese greed as well," he interposed.

Of course he was right. Mobutu had acquired fabulous wealth and ruined his country in consequence.

Gerard Pambu is my age – seventy. He'd been living in the Congo at the same time as us. But, as we both agreed, we would never have met in those days. We talked about his upbringing. His father, an évolué, had been a headmaster with only three years of education. Gerard, however, had been sent to a Catholic seminary and had gone on to study at Lovanium, a university in Léopoldville established in 1954. He had then gone to America on a scholarship to study for his PhD.

"It was education," he explained. "The Belgians hoped that by denying us secondary education they could keep us down for ever. But some of our évolués went to the conference in Brussels just before Independence and came across people like Nyerere and Nkomo, who were far better educated than they were. It was then that they realised how much they had been denied. They were humiliated. That was why Lumumba denounced the Belgian government in his inauguration speech."

"And the greed?" I asked.

"Oh yes, we too are guilty." Gerard went on to explain that the present atrocities in the Eastern Congo are partly due to the presence of a mineral called coltan. An essential ingredient for mobile phones and other electronic products, coltan is found in the Eastern Congo, close to Rwanda, where earlier Belgian interference had contributed to the conflict between Hutus and Tutsis and the Rwandan genocide.

I told Gerard what a BBC reporter had said in the nineties: "There is absolutely no infrastructure left in Kinshasa (Léopoldville). No roads, no telephones, nothing." But I told him, too, about the hope she expressed: "And yet, there is something happening in le marché. It's as if there's some spark of new life being born in the marketplace."

"It is true," Gerard confirmed. "You cannot imagine the degree of poverty in the Congo at the moment. People are having to live on very little. There is no medication, so people are going back to the villages to find the traditional plants and leaves that have healing powers. In the marketplace you see people using every kind of human ingenuity to survive."

I like that. I have always liked the idea of a phoenix rising from the ashes of a fire.

THE END

I would like to thank my son, Charles,
for urging me to write this book,
my daughter Jessica for reading the manuscript,
and my friend Dawn Garisch
for telling me to send it to Kwela Books.

VERONICA CECIL was born in India during the time of the British Raj. She has lived in the former Rhodesia, in South Africa and the Congo, but these days spends most of her time in the UK. Formerly a writer of radio and television plays, she became a radio journalist after the death of her husband. She is a mother of four and grandmother of nine.